The Mediterranean Diet Cookbook

A Step-By-Step Guide To Quick, Easy, And Low-Budget Mediterranean Recipes For Weight Loss. Everything You Need To Know About The Mediterranean Diet.

Randon Scott B.

The Mediterranean Diet Cookbook

© Copyright 2021 - All rights reserved.

The content contained within this book may not be reproduced, duplicated or transmitted without direct written permission from the author or the publisher.

Under no circumstances will any blame or legal responsibility be held against the publisher, or author, for any damages, reparation, or monetary loss due to the information contained within this book. Either directly or indirectly.

Legal Notice:

This book is copyright protected. This book is only for personal use. You cannot amend, distribute, sell, use, quote or paraphrase any part, or the content within this book, without the consent of the author or publisher.

Disclaimer Notice:

Please note the information contained within this document is for educational and entertainment purposes only. All effort has been executed to present accurate, up to date, and reliable, complete information. No warranties of any kind are declared or implied. Readers acknowledge that the author is not engaging in the rendering of legal, financial, medical or professional advice. The content within this book has been derived from various sources. Please consult a licensed professional before attempting any techniques outlined in this book.

By reading this document, the reader agrees that under no circumstances is the author responsible for any losses, direct or indirect, which are incurred as a result of the use of information contained within this document, including, but not limited to, errors, omissions, or inaccuracies.

The Mediterranean Diet Cookbook

Table of Contents

INTRODUCTION 8

CHAPTER 1. HEALTH BENEFITS OF THE MEDITERRANEAN DIET 12

- LOWERS RISK OF CARDIOVASCULAR DISEASE 12
- IMPROVES HEART HEALTH 12
- WEIGHT LOSS 13
- CAN HELP TO FIGHT CANCER 13
- PROTECTS COGNITIVE HEALTH... 14
- INCREASE YOUR LIFESPAN! 15
- PROTECTION AGAINST TYPE-2 DIABETES 15
- IMPROVES SEX LIFE.. 16
- INCREASE SIGHT 16
- YOUR KIDNEY FUNCTION IMPROVES 17
- KEEPS YOUR SKIN HEALTHY 17
- MEAT CONSUMPTION... 20
- RED WINE CONSUMPTION... 20
- FRUITS AND VEGETABLES.. 23
- SPICES AND OILS 24

CHAPTER 2. HOW DO I START A MEDITERRANEAN DIET? .. 28

- FOOD TO EAT 28
- FOOD TO AVOID.. 30

CHAPTER 3. TOP TIPS 32

- NEVER SKIP BREAKFAST 32
- WHEN DINING OUT.. 32
- CHOP YOUR VEGETABLES... 33
- SHOP LOCALLY.. 33
- KEEP NUTS & SEEDS.. 33
- EAT SLOWER.. 33
- USE WHOLE GRAINS... 34
- MANAGE PORTIONS... 34

CHAPTER 4. BREAKFAST RECIPES 36

1. COLORFUL BACON AND BRIE OMELETTE WEDGES 36
2. PEARL COUSCOUS SALAD 38
3. SIMPLE COCONUT PORRIDGE 41
4. CRUMBLED FETA AND SCALLIONS.. 43

5. EARLY MORNING QUINOA CHICKEN SALAD 45
6. VEGETABLE QUINOA 48
7. QUINOA BREAKFAST BOWLS 50
8. DELICIOUS BREAKFAST POTATO MIX... 52
9. PERFECT BREAKFAST OATMEAL 54
10. MIX BERRY OATMEAL 56
11. WARM PUMPKIN OATS 58
12. BLUEBERRY BREAKFAST OATMEAL 60
13. PEAR OATMEAL 61

CHAPTER 6. LUNCH RECIPES 64

14. PUMPKIN PIE PARFAIT 64
15. MEDITERRANEAN EGGS (SHAKSHUKA) 66
16. MORNING OVERNIGHT OATS WITH RASPBERRIES 69
17. SCRAMBLE EGGS WITH TOMATOES 71
18. BAKED EGGS IN AVOCADO 73
19. EGGPLANT PARMESAN... 75
20. MUSHROOM PASTILLA 77
21. FAVA BEANS AND RICE 80

CHAPTER 8. SNACKS RECIPES.. 82

22. MARINATED OLIVES 82
23. PICKLED TURNIPS 84
24. BRAISED SWEET PEPPERS... 86
25. CARAMELIZED PEARL ONIONS 88
26. PATATAS BRAVAS... 90
27. FILO-WRAPPED BRIE WITH ORANGE MARMALADE.................. 92
28. BUTTERED FAVA BEANS 94
29. FRIED RICE BALLS WITH TOMATO SAUCE............................... 96
30. SAVORY MEDITERRANEAN POPCORN 99
31. TURKISH-SPICED NUTS 101
32. LEMONY ORZO 103
33. PUFF PASTRY TURNOVER WITH ROASTED VEGETABLES 105
34. TURMERIC-SPICED CRUNCHY CHICKPEAS.............................. 107
35. -CRISPY GARLIC OVEN POTATOES 110

CHAPTER 10. DINNER RECIPES 112

36. NAKED LASAGNA 112
37. GNOCCHI, TOMATOES, AND PANCETTA 114
38. PENNE AND CHICKEN 116
39. SPINACH AND FETA PITA BAKE 118

40.	Mediterranean Flounder	120
41.	Greek Olive and Feta Cheese Pasta	122
42.	Tomatoes Stuffed With Goat Cheese	124
43.	Cucumber Yogurt Salad	126
44.	Savory Greek White Fava Bean Salad	128
45.	Tangy Orange Roasted Asparagus Salad	130
46.	Mediterranean Mixed Greens	132
47.	Creamy Paninis	134

CHAPTER 13. DRINKS RECIPES 136

48.	Turkish Coffee Almond Frappé	136
49.	Moroccan Mint Tea	138
50.	Chamomile Lemon Honey Iced Tea	140
51.	Pomegranate Berry Sangria	142
52.	Raspberry Fizz Cocktail	144
53.	Chocolate Banana Smoothie	146
54.	Fruit Smoothie	148
55.	Mango-Pear Smoothie	149
56.	Strawberry-Rhubarb Smoothie	151
57.	Chia-Pomegranate Smoothie	153
58.	Sweet Kale Smoothie	155
59.	Avocado-Blueberry Smoothie	157

CONCLUSION 160

The Mediterranean Diet Cookbook

Introduction

The Mediterranean diet is inspired by the eating habits of the populations that surround the Mediterranean Sea. The populations of southern Italy and Greece are the main regions that influence this diet. It isn't the diet consumed today in many of these regions that gained so much attention. The Mediterranean diet refers to the traditional eating habits and lifestyles of these areas in the 1950s and 1960s. During this time, researchers noticed a significant difference in populations' health in these areas compared to those living in America. Many of the Mediterranean areas were healthier. The key difference between those living in the Mediterranean and those living in America was their diet.

The Harvard School of Public Health and the Athens Medical School in Greece conducted a study in 2003 that indicated those following a Mediterranean diet had longer lifespans (rock ridge Press, 2013). Another study in 2008 focused on how the Mediterranean diet could help individuals lose weight (rock ridge Press, 2013). Even more striking is that those who follow a Mediterranean diet have significantly lowered their risk of heart disease and cognitive decline, diabetes, and mental health issues (rock ridge Press, 2013). Research continues today, showing how eating a rich diet in fresh fruits, vegetables, healthy fat, and whole grains, like the Mediterranean diet, can drastically improve one's health. There are hundreds of case studies and research data showing how switching to a Mediterranean diet can reduce heart disease risk, considered the leading cause of death in America. It has been shown to reduce the effect of diabetes and help prevent cognitive decline.

Despite all the evidence that points out the Mediterranean diet's undeniable benefits, not everyone is quick to follow the Mediterranean diet. In fact, individuals living in the Mediterranean today do not even follow the traditional way of life that made the area one of the world's healthiest just a few decades ago.

There is a great deal of debate about some of the Mediterranean diet components that twist the facts. Eating healthy fats is one of the most attacked aspects of the Mediterranean diet. For a while, all fats were looked at as bad because there was little understanding of the various forms of fats the body could use for energy; this is also true of carbohydrates. What Ancel Keys discovered and many other researchers was that the fats consumed with the Mediterranean diet differed greatly from the fats being consumed in excess in the United States. It was healthy fats like olive oil that was one of the biggest contributors to individuals' optimal health.

Another misconception was red meat. People believed that cutting out red meat from one's diet was unhealthy. Red meat was supposed to be one of the only forms of protein you could eat, and eating red meat only occasionally was the opposite of what the United States Department of Agriculture was suggesting.

The Mediterranean Diet Cookbook

Chapter 1. Health Benefits of the Mediterranean Diet

Lowers Risk of Cardiovascular Disease

The Mediterranean diet has been recognized to be most helpful in reducing high triglyceride levels. Triglycerides are fatty molecules that travel throughout the bloodstream and build up plaque in our arteries. A higher triglyceride count or its accumulation in the bloodstream and vessels can lead to higher cholesterol and an increased risk of stroke or heart attack. Even though the Mediterranean diet consists of fatty items like olive oil and salmon, they are good fats loaded with beneficial monounsaturated and polyunsaturated fats.

The Mediterranean diet proves more effective at reducing high triglyceride counts, while still maintaining "good" cholesterol (or HDL cholesterol) in the blood.

Improves Heart Health

The study shows that a Mediterranean diet rich in ALA (alpha-linolenic acid) found in olive oil can decrease cardiac death risk in a person by nearly 30. Further research shows that when comparing the blood pressure between people who consumed sunflower oil versus those consuming extra virgin oil, the olive oil consumers could decrease their blood pressure by more significant amounts.

It might seem counterintuitive that olive oil can lower blood pressure. Still, the peculiarity of virgin olive oil is to be an unrefined oil, which means that the plant additions are intact and can improve cellular function. By adding this with the healthy fats consumed in the Mediterranean diet, it will surely allow your body to slowly decrease the amount of unhealthy triglycerides you are consuming to improve overall heart health.

Weight Loss

The types of food that the Mediterranean diet encourages, such as whole grains, beans, and legumes, contain high amounts of fiber, which help to slow digestion and prevent frequent spikes in blood sugar levels. That means you feel full for a longer period without needing a snack.

Blood sugar spikes are dangerous to our body because in order to contrast them, the body is forced to produce high amounts of insulin, a hormone that causes weight gain. Also, fibers in contact with water become swollen and contribute to increased satiety, thereby preventing you from eating more food than necessary.

Mediterranean diet is less caloric than the fatty diet of many western countries. It makes large use of aromatic herbs that allow you to flavour the dishes, which has little or no amounts of fatty and high-calorie condiments.

Can Help to Fight Cancer

Of course, there's no cure for cancer. Still, studies have found that the Mediterranean diet provides the most favorable conditions for the body to fight against cancer. A 2013 study at the University of Genoa in Italy found that the Mediterranean diet provides your body with a balanced ratio of omega fatty acids, fiber, and antioxidants found in wine, fruits, vegetables, and olive oil. Providing high amounts of antioxidants is the key to fighting cancer cells and stopping further cell mutation.

A study at the Mayo Clinic found that 800 people with advanced colon polyps ate red meat more frequently, and their diet did not correspond to foods on the Mediterranean diet. The World Cancer Research Fund reports that eating at least 90 grams of whole grains a day can reduce your risk of colon cancer by almost 20%. This is because the fiber in whole grains prevents any mutations from developing in your digestive tract and keeps your bowel movement in check.

Protects Cognitive Health

Following the Mediterranean diet could be key in protecting yourself from future neurodegenerative diseases like Parkinson's, dementia, or Alzheimer's. The healthy fats that the Mediterranean diet is full of are known to fight age-related cognitive decline, along with the anti-inflammatory protection that fresh fruits and vegetables provide.

The Taube Institute for Research in Alzheimer's disease found that the more strictly the individuals in their test group followed the Mediterranean diet, the lower their risk for developing Alzheimer's disease. Doctors have always encouraged seniors and patients at risk for neurodegenerative diseases to adopt healthier eating habits to delay or inhibit their dementia symptoms. Following a Mediterranean diet can improve your memory, mental acuity, and attention span as it protects your nerve cells from deteriorating with age.

Increase Your Lifespan!

A famous research called the Lyon Diet Heart Study tested a group of individuals who had heart attacks between 1988 and 1992. They were counseled to follow a traditional post-heart attack diet or the Mediterranean diet.

When a follow-up study was conducted over 4 years, the results found that the people following the Mediterranean diet had a reduced heart disease risk by 70%. They also experienced a nearly 50% lower risk of death than the standard low-fat diet. The combination of fresh fruits and vegetables and healthy fat sources like beans, nuts, and fish are a winning combination to extend the human lifespan.

Protection Against Type-2 Diabetes

With the Mediterranean diet, you limit yourself to eat less processed food. The fat your body absorbs is mostly from olive oil, nuts, and healthy meats. It's not a "low carb" diet, but still reduces the amount of your carbohydrate intake so that fewer cars are converted to glucose. A 2011 study in Spain discovered that over 4-year research, participants assigned to a Mediterranean-style diet had a reduced risk of developing Type 2 diabetes by more than 50%. The result showed massive progress compared to the other group that followed a low-fat diet.

The Mediterranean diet encourages meals seasoned with healthy spices and encourages you to fill your dessert with fruit instead of baked foods containing sugar. In many studies, it is also important to note that participants on the Mediterranean diet tended to lose on average more weight than participants on other low carb or low-fat diets. Due to this weight loss, you can reduce your diabetes risk and maybe even delay needing any further medication.

Improves Sex Life

Erectile dysfunction or ED, is a common side effect of cardiovascular disease. As the blood vessels are blocked with unhealthy plaque, the smaller vessels leading towards the male genitalia cannot respond like they used to. But research shows that the Mediterranean diet can help with this too!

Increase Sight

Since the Mediterranean diet is full of fruits, vegetables, and regular fish servings, it has great amounts of vitamins that protect your sight. According to the American Academy of Ophthalmology, eye health is protected by eating antioxidants found in fresh plant products. Fish is also high in omega 3 fatty acids, which is critical to sight health. Just having one serving of fish in a week can lower the risk of developing eye damage, which occurs commonly in people over 50. With the Mediterranean diet, you are incorporating fish in your diet more than two times a week! The seeds and nuts you are eating as snacks also contain fatty acids that protect the retinas from cellular damage, which occurs with age.

Your Kidney Function Improves

Your kidneys are constantly working throughout the day to filter waste and liquid from your body while still maintaining your blood pressure. But chronic kidney disease can affect more than 30 million Americans a year.

A 2014 study in the Clinical Journal of American Society of Nephrology found that following the Mediterranean diet may decrease the chances of having chronic kidney disease by almost 50%. This could be attributed to clean and healthy food choices that the Mediterranean diet requires, with less processed food and red meat. Fish, nuts, fresh fruits, and vegetables are known to lower inflammation in the body, which causes kidney disease.

Keeps Your Skin Healthy

A diet rich in antioxidants found in fresh fruits and vegetables helps to keep your skin at its healthiest. That means healthy growth, strong elasticity, and prevention against common skin conditions like eczema, acne, or rosacea. One of the worst foods for your skin is sugar, which can cause inflammation in our body, thus contributing to collagen breakdown. This helpful protein keeps the skin firm.

Chapter 2. Benefits of the Most Used Products in the Mediterranean Fish

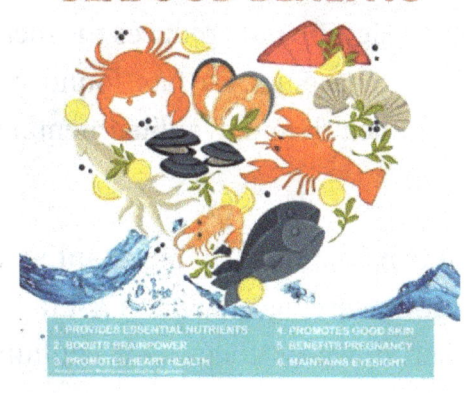

We have talked quite a bit about fish consumption on the Mediterranean diet, and my point of view is that you really can't eat enough fish and seafood. Eating more fish and seafood can help to improve your intake of nutrients. For example, most fish contains significant amounts of iodine. If you are not using a salt product with added iodine, you might be deficient in this important element that is critical for the proper functioning of the thyroid. Fish also contains many other important vitamins and minerals. For example, fish is an excellent vitamin D source. In fact, nearly every type of seafood, from shrimp to salmon, contains some level of vitamin D. Fish also contains potassium and magnesium. If you can stomach the taste, canned fish like sardines contains a good amount of calcium from the bones. This might shock you—but fish is even a source of vitamin C. An average-sized half-filet of salmon can give you 12% of your daily RDA of vitamin C.

The main benefit of eating fish comes from eating fatty fish, which contains large amounts of omega-3 fats. It now turns out that taking omega-3 supplements does not convey many health benefits as had been hoped; however, it is scientifically proven that consuming fish significantly reduces the incidence of heart disease and stroke. The omega-3 fats found in fish are also important for brain health and avoiding mental problems like depression.

But what isn't in fish is almost as important as what's in fish. For example, a 200g serving of salmon contains 27 grams of fat. This is broken down as follows—it contains 6 grams of saturated fat, 8 grams of polyunsaturated fat (mostly omega 3), and 7 grams of heart-healthy monounsaturated fat.

Let's compare this to a 300 g serving of rib-eye steak. It's not that rib-eye steak doesn't contain important nutrients, it certainly does. This serving of rib-eye steak would supply you with 70% of your vitamin B6, 16% of your magnesium, and 757 mg of potassium. It even contains 31 grams of monounsaturated fats. However, it also contains 28 grams of saturated fats. As a proportion, it contains a lot more saturated fat than salmon and other fatty fish do. And that is the difference that makes beef less heart-healthy than fish.

Meat Consumption

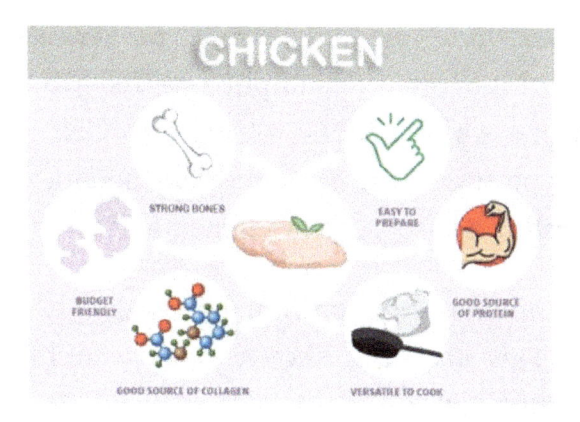

As noted in the last section, red meat does contain a large number of nutrients. Pork and poultry products contain large amounts of nutrients as well. However, due to the saturated fat content, remember that you should generally limit your intake of meat as compared to other components of the Mediterranean diet. Like beef, chicken also includes a large supply of minerals like potassium and magnesium.

Red Wine Consumption

So we know that red wine seems to impart some health benefits, including a reduction in the rates of heart attack and stroke, but how does it do it? Probably one way is that moderate alcohol consumption can contribute to the decrease in overall stress levels. Moderate consumption of red wine can lower blood pressure, which may be related to the alcohol's stress-reducing properties when consumed in moderation. But the benefits of red wine are more fundamental than that.

Red wine contains an important antioxidant that is called resveratrol. This has been shown to have multiple positive effects throughout the body, including protecting cardiovascular health and reducing the risk of many cancers. It can also help protect against vision loss and UV radiation. It has recently been found that red wine also contains procyanidins substances. These chemicals can help maintain healthy blood vessels.

It has also been found that resveratrol influences the size of tumors of the colon. It is not clear that regular consumption of red wine could reduce the incidence of colon cancer. Still, it has been shown that resveratrol can reduce tumor size, and so it appears to inhibit the growth of colon cancer cells. Red wine has also been thought to play a role in reducing risks associated with breast, lung, and prostate cancer.

Several studies have also tied regular red wine consumption to a lower risk of dementia. Two effects of red wine appear to play a role here. These actions may also explain why red wine, when consumed regularly and in moderation, may reduce heart attack and stroke risk. First off, red wine reduces the stickiness of platelets in the blood, making the formation of clots less likely. Red wine also helps to keep blood vessels open and flexible. This makes strokes and clots leading to heart attacks less likely, and it generally keeps blood vessels healthier. Interestingly, high blood pressure has the opposite effect, making blood vessels stiffen and become less flexible. These factors are also thought to help keep a good blood supply to the brain. They may, in part, explain why a Mediterranean diet containing regular consumption of red wine reduces the risks of dementia.

Another interesting effect of red wine consumption is that it may inhibit fatty liver disease. One reason this is interesting is that consuming alcohol regularly will raise your risk of developing fatty liver disease.

If you have problems with drinking alcohol, it's best to avoid it. But otherwise, moderate consumption of red wine regularly can impart many health benefits. Remember that it must be steady and moderate doses. So two glasses a

The day is not something you are attaining if you consume two bottles one night!.

Fruits and Vegetables

FRUIT AND VEGETABLES BENEFITS

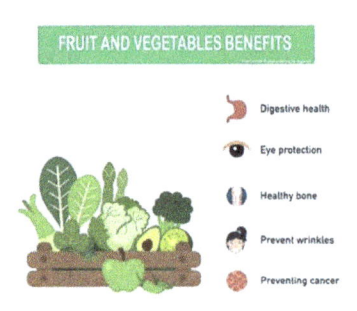

- Digestive health
- Eye protection
- Healthy bone
- Prevent wrinkles
- Preventing cancer

The regular consumption of fruits and vegetables is an important component of the Mediterranean diet. As we described in the last chapter, you should fill about half your plate with fruits and vegetables. One way I like to do it is to fill half of the plate with vegetables and then eat fruits as a dessert item. Fruits also make a good component of snacks, although you should supplement them with nuts and cheese to not have a sugar-laden snack by itself that could raise your blood sugar.

The nutritional benefits of fruits and vegetables are well established. A large component of your Mediterranean diet should include leafy green vegetables. These include spinach, mustard greens, romaine lettuce, and any other kind of green. You can also add broccoli and cabbage to the list. These types of vegetables contain many important micronutrients and vitamins. For example, they contain vitamins A and C. Vitamin K. Vitamin K1 is important for proper blood clotting. Vitamin K2 is important for keeping calcium out of your blood vessels (the process of calcification helps create "hardened arteries" that lead to heart disease). Green vegetables can also help you maintain eye health, as they contain the chemicals lutein and zeaxanthin, both of which have been shown to help reduce the risk of macular degeneration.

Vegetables are also a good source of many important minerals. These include potassium, calcium, and magnesium. Many people in western countries don't realize this, but they are deficient in magnesium. This can cause problems with muscles and heart arrhythmias. Low levels of magnesium can also lead to high blood pressure in some people.

Spices and Oils

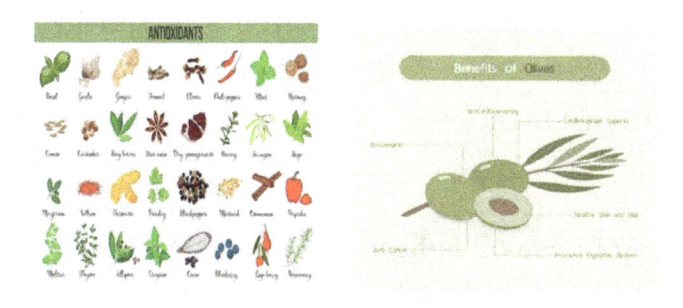

Of course, we have emphasized the importance of extra virgin olive oil throughout the book. Olive oil helps you maintain a healthy cardiovascular system, reduce inflammation and cancer risk, cut the risk of heart attack and stroke, and maintain healthy cholesterol levels. One surprising benefit of olive oil that we haven't mentioned is that it contains a polyunsaturated fat called omega-7, which is only recently recognized as important for heart health.

Remember that high triglycerides and high LDL cholesterol both significantly increase the risk of heart disease and stroke. Fish oil will lower triglyceride levels if you eat enough fish. This generally means eating one serving of fatty fish per day. But there is a way to lower LDL cholesterol—and that is by consuming omega-7 fatty acids. You can do that by consuming olive oil and avocados.

In addition to all of these benefits, olive oil is believed to help reduce the risk of Alzheimer's disease and other dementias. It probably does this by reducing inflammation and ensuring a good supply of blood to the brain.

The ability of olive oil to act as an anti-inflammatory is also impactful for many other, sometimes surprising health conditions. For example, it may reduce the risk of ulcerative colitis and assist in recovery with patients who have developed pancreatitis.

About 73% of olive oil is heart-healthy monounsaturated fat. This is in the form of a healthy compound called oleic acid. But that is not the only healthy component of olive oil. We already mentioned that it contains omega-7 fatty acids. Still, olive oil also contains vitamins E and K. In fact, a tablespoon of olive oil will supply 13% of your daily recommended dosage of vitamin E. Although the research is not settled, it is believed by many medical professionals that vitamin E may play a role in the prevention of dementia, and this also helps to explain why olive oil would provide many health benefits, among these reducing the risk of dementia.

Many spices are used in the Mediterranean diet, and these go well beyond simply providing enhanced tastes. Common spices used in the Mediterranean diet include fennel, coriander, cumin, bay leaf, basil, and dill. Sage, thyme, saffron, and rosemary are also commonly used. Many of these spices were introduced into European cuisine by contact with Arab traders. These spices can play a role in your health and, if consumed regularly and may help reduce the risk of cancer, inflammation, and other health conditions. Turmeric can also be used in some Mediterranean dishes. This versatile and flavorful spice has been associated with many health benefits due to its anti-inflammatory properties.

The Mediterranean Diet Cookbook

Chapter 2. How Do I Start a Mediterranean Diet?

Mediterranean diet is based on easy to find ingredients that are rich in vitamins, nutrients, and antioxidants. It is one of the budget-friendly diet plans with few limitations. During the diet period, you can eat all kinds of vegetables, an adequate amount of eggs, poultry, yogurt, cheese, sour cream, and heavy cream and avoid meat, refined oil, sweetened beverages, and processed foods.

Food to Eat

Fruits and Vegetables

Mediterranean diet is one of the plant-based diet plans. Fresh fruits and vegetables contain a large number of vitamins, nutrients, fibers, minerals, and antioxidants

Fruits: Apple, berries, grapes, peaches, fig, grapefruit, dates, melon, oranges, and pears.

Vegetables: Spinach, Brussels sprout, kale, tomatoes, kale, summer squash, onion, cauliflower, peppers, cucumbers, turnips, potatoes, sweet potatoes, and parsnips.

Seeds and Nuts

Seeds and nuts are rich in monounsaturated fats and omega-3 fatty acids.

Seeds: pumpkin seeds, flax seeds, sesame seeds, and sunflower seeds.

Nuts: Almond, hazelnuts, pistachios, cashews, and walnuts.

Whole Grains

Whole grains are high in fibers, and they are not processed, so they do not contain unhealthy fats as trans-fats compare to processed ones.

Whole grains: Wheat, quinoa, rice, barley, oats, rye, and brown rice. You can also use bread and pasta, which is made from whole grains.

Fish and Seafood

Fish are a rich source of omega-3 fatty acids and proteins. Eating fish at least once a week is recommended here. The healthiest way to consume fish is to grill it. Grilling fish taste good and never need extra oil.

Fish and seafood: salmon, trout, clams, mackerel, sardines, tuna, and shrimp.

Legumes

Legumes (beans) are a rich source of protein, vitamins, and fibers. Regular consumption of beans helps to reduce the risk of diabetes, cancer, and heart disease.

Legumes: Kidney beans, peas, chickpeas, black beans, fava beans, lentils, and pinto beans.

Spices and Herbs

Spices and herbs are used to add taste to your meal.

Spices and herbs: mint, thyme, garlic, basil, cinnamon, nutmeg, rosemary, oregano and more.

Healthy Fats

Olive oil is the main fat used in the Mediterranean diet. It helps to reduce the risk of inflammatory disorder, diabetes, cancer, and heart-related disease. It also increases HDL (good cholesterol) levels and decreases LDL (bad cholesterol) levels in your body. It also helps to lose weight.

Fats: Olive oil, avocado oil, walnut oil, extra virgin olive oil, avocado, and olives.

Dairy

Moderate amounts of dairy products are allowed during the Mediterranean diet. The dairy product contains high amounts of fats.

Dairy: Greek yogurt, skim milk, and cheese.

Food to Avoid

Refined Grains

Refined grains are not allowed in a Mediterranean diet. It raises your blood sugar level—refined grains like light bread, polished rice, and pasta.

Refined Oils

The Mediterranean diet completely avoids oils like vegetable oils, cottonseed oils, and soybean oils. It raises your LDL (bad cholesterol) level.

Added Sugar

Added sugar is not allowed in the Mediterranean diet. These artificial sugars are found in table sugar, soda, chocolate, ice cream, and candies. It raises your blood sugar level. You should consume only natural sugars in the Mediterranean diet.

Chapter 3. Top Tips

You already know that starting a new diet can be hard, and the Mediterranean diet is no different. Here are some top tips so that you can be successful with your dietary change.

Never Skip Breakfast

When dieting, skipping a meal can seem like a good idea, but it isn't. Breakfast is one of the most commonly skipped meals because it's easier for you to wait for lunch than for someone to wait for dinner if they skip lunch. Though skipping any meal can put your metabolism behind schedule. It's better to keep your refrigerator stocked with fruit and yogurt for small, light breakfasts that are also great on the go.

When Dining Out

You aren't going to be able to stop going out to eat just because you're on a diet, especially when it's going to be a lifestyle change. Of course, you should try to limit dining out whenever possible for the first month of your lifestyle change. However, when you do go out to eat, start by dividing your meal in half. Don't wait either. You'll want to divide your plate the moment it comes to you. Save half for later, so ask for a take-out container if at all possible. It's unlikely that you'll have food that fits your diet when eating out, so limiting your portion control is the first step in making sure you don't blow all of the hard work you've put in.

Chop Your Vegetables

It's best to chop your vegetables in advance so that you can use them for snacks and quick lunches. Some of the best vegetables to keep on hand for this is bell peppers, celery, carrots, and cucumbers. They're also perfect for dipping in hummus, which is a healthy snack too!

Shop Locally

You may want to pay a visit to your local farmer's market as well. It's a great way to keep your house stocked full of seasonal vegetables that are sure to be fresh. It can also help to cut costs if you're shopping locally and seasonally. You shouldn't let your budget be your downfall when making an important lifestyle change, and shopping locally sourced food can help.

Keep Nuts & Seeds

It's just as important that you keep nuts and seeds on hand for a healthy alternative to chips, cookies and other processed foods. Some great choices are sunflower seeds, almonds or walnuts. Remember that these shouldn't be salted either!

Eat Slower

You should savor your food if you want to make sure you aren't rushing through and eating more than you need to. If you cherish your time eating by sharing it with family and friends, you will eat slower and consume fewer calories. You're also more likely to want to put in the extra effort to make a healthy, tasty meal, making it take some time. That's why getting your family involved is also a healthful tip.

Use Whole Grains

You already know that whole grains are an essential part of the Mediterranean diet, so you need to switch to them for success. Minimally processed grains are healthier, including couscous, bulgur, barley, oats rice, polenta, faro, and millet.

Manage Portions

The Mediterranean diet encourages portion control. Don't concentrate on counting calories. Instead, you need to concentrate on the quality of calories that you're eating. Calories are important, but your calorie type is much more important. This diet has nutrient-dense food that will help you to stay full in the long run, so you don't have to eat a large amount of it. Always keep an eye on your plate size if you want to stay on track.

The Mediterranean Diet Cookbook

Chapter 4. Breakfast Recipes

1. Colorful Bacon and Brie Omelette Wedges

- ✓ **Preparation Time: 10 minutes**
- ✓ **Cooking Time: 10 minutes**
- ✓ **Servings: 6**

Ingredients:

- 2 tablespoons olive oil
- 7 ounces smoked bacon
- 6 beaten eggs
- Small bunch chives, snipped
- 3 ½ ounces brie, sliced
- 1 teaspoon red wine vinegar
- 1 teaspoon Dijon mustard
- 1 cucumber, halved, deseeded, and sliced diagonally

- 7 ounces radish, quartered

Directions:

1. Turn your grill on and set it to high.

2. Take a small-sized pan and add 1 teaspoon of oil; allow the oil to heat up.

3. Add lardons and fry until crisp.

4. Drain the lardon on kitchen paper.

5. Take another non-stick cast iron frying pan and place it over grill, heat 2 teaspoons of oil.

6. Add lardons, eggs, chives, ground pepper to the frying pan. Cook on LOW until they are semi-set.

7. Carefully lay brie on top and grill until the Brie sets and is a golden texture. Remove it from the pan and cut up into wedges. Take a small bowl and create dressing by mixing olive oil, mustard, vinegar and seasoning.

8. Add cucumber to the bowl and mix, serve alongside the Omelette wedges.

9. Enjoy!

Nutrition: Calories: 35g Fat: 31g Carbohydrates: 3g Protein: 25g

2. Pearl Couscous Salad

- ✓ **Preparation Time: 15 minutes**
- ✓ **Cooking Time: 0 minutes**
- ✓ **Servings: 6**

Ingredients:

- For Lemon Dill Vinaigrette
- Juice of 1 large sized lemon
- 1/3 cup of extra virgin olive oil
- 1 teaspoon of dill weed
- 1 teaspoon of garlic powder
- Salt as needed
- Pepper
- For Israeli Couscous

- 2 cups of Pearl Couscous
- Extra virgin olive oil
- 2 cups of halved grape tomatoes
- Water as needed
- 1/3 cup of finely chopped red onions
- ½ of a finely chopped English cucumber
- 15 ounces of chickpeas
- 14 ounce can of artichoke hearts (roughly chopped up)
- ½ cup of pitted Kalamata olives
- 15-20 pieces of fresh basil leaves, roughly torn and chopped up
- 3 ounces of fresh baby mozzarella

Directions:

1. Prepare the vinaigrette by taking a bowl and add the ingredients listed under vinaigrette.
2. Mix them well and keep aside.
3. Take a medium-sized heavy pot and place it over medium heat.
4. Add 2 tablespoons of olive oil and allow it to heat up.

5. Add couscous and keep cooking until golden brown.

6. Add 3 cups of boiling water and cook the couscous according to the package instructions.

7. Once done, drain in a colander and keep aside.

8. Take another large-sized mixing bowl and add the remaining ingredients except the cheese and basil.

9. Add the cooked couscous and basil to the mix and mix everything well.

10. Give the vinaigrette a nice stir and whisk it into the couscous salad.

11. Mix well.

12. Adjust the seasoning as required.

13. Add mozzarella cheese.

14. Garnish with some basil.

15. Enjoy!

Nutrition:

- Calories: 393
- Fat: 13g
- Carbohydrates: 57g Protein: 13g

3. Simple Coconut Porridge

- ✓ **Preparation Time:** 15 minutes
- ✓ **Cooking Time:** Nil
- ✓ **Servings:** 6

Ingredients:

- Powdered erythritol as needed
- 1 ½ cups almond milk, unsweetened
- 2 tablespoons protein powder
- 3 tablespoons Golden Flaxseed meal
- 2 tablespoons coconut flour

Directions:

1. Take a bowl and mix in flaxseed meal, protein powder, coconut flour and mix well.
2. Add mix to saucepan (placed over medium heat).

3. Add almond milk and stir, let the mixture thicken.

4. Add your desired amount of sweetener and serve.

5. Enjoy!

Nutrition:

- Calories: 259 g
- Fat: 13g
- Carbohydrates: 5g
- Protein: 16g

4. Crumbled Feta and Scallions

- ✓ **Preparation Time: 5 minutes**
- ✓ **Cooking Time: 15 minutes**
- ✓ **Servings: 12**

Ingredients:

- 2 tablespoons of unsalted butter (replace with canola oil for full effect)
- ½ cup of chopped up scallions
- 1 cup of crumbled feta cheese
- 8 large sized eggs
- 2/3 cup of milk
- ½ teaspoon of dried Italian seasoning
- Salt as needed
- Freshly ground black pepper as needed

- Cooking oil spray

Directions:

1. Preheat your oven to 400 º Fahrenheit.
2. Take a 3-4 ounce muffin pan and grease with cooking oil.
3. Take a non-stick pan and place it over medium heat.
4. Add butter and allow the butter to melt.
5. Add half of the scallions and stir fry.
6. Keep them to the side.
7. Take a medium-sized bowl and add eggs, Italian seasoning and milk and whisk well.
8. Add the stir fried scallions and feta cheese and mix.
9. Season with pepper and salt.
10. Pour the mix into the muffin tin.
11. Transfer the muffin tin to your oven and bake for 15 minutes.
12. Serve with a sprinkle of scallions. Enjoy!

Nutrition: Calories: 106 gFat: 8g Carbohydrates: 2g Protein: 7g

5. Early Morning Quinoa Chicken Salad

✓ **Preparation Time: 15 minutes**

✓ **Cooking Time: 20 minutes**

✓ **Servings: 8**

Ingredients:

- 2 cups of water //
- 2 cubes of chicken bouillon
- 1 smashed garlic clove
- 1 cup of uncooked quinoa
- 2 large sized chicken breast cut up into bite-sized portions and cooked
- 1 large sized diced red onion
- 1 large sized green bell pepper
- ½ cup of Kalamata olives

- ½ cup of crumbled feta cheese
- ¼ cup of chopped up parsley
- ¼ cup of chopped up fresh chives
- ½ teaspoon of salt
- 1 tablespoon of balsamic vinegar
- ¼ cup of olive oil

Directions:

1. Take a saucepan and bring your water, garlic, and bouillon cubes to a boil.
2. Stir in quinoa and reduce the heat to medium-low.
3. Simmer for about 15-20 minutes until the quinoa has absorbed all the water and is tender.
4. Discard your garlic cloves and scrape the quinoa into a large-sized bowl.
5. Gently stir in the cooked chicken breast, bell pepper, onion, feta cheese, chives, salt and parsley into your quinoa.
6. Drizzle some lemon juice, olive oil, and balsamic vinegar.
7. Stir everything until mixed well.

8. Serve warm and enjoy!

Nutrition:

- Calories: 99 g
- Fat: 7g
- Carbohydrates: 7g
- Protein: 3.4g

6. Vegetable Quinoa

- ✓ **Preparation Time: 10 minutes**
- ✓ **Cooking Time: 1 minute**
- ✓ **Servings: 6**

Ingredients:

- 1 cup quinoa, rinsed and drained
- 1 1/2 cups water
- 4 cups spinach, chopped
- 1 bell pepper, chopped
- 2 carrots, chopped
- 1 celery stalk, chopped
- 1/3 cup feta cheese, crumbled
- 1/2 cup olives, sliced

- 1/3 cup pesto
- 2 tomatoes, chopped
- Pepper
- Salt

Directions:

1. Add quinoa, spinach, bell pepper, carrots, celery, water, pepper, and salt into the instant pot and stir well.
2. Seal pot with lid and cook on high for 1 minute.
3. Once done, allow to release pressure naturally for 10 minutes then release remaining using quick release. Remove lid.
4. Add remaining ingredients and stir everything well.
5. Serve and enjoy.

Nutrition:

- Calories: 226
- Fat: 10.7 g
- Carbohydrates: 26 g
- Sugar: 4.4 g
- Protein: 7.9 g Cholesterol: 11 mg

7. Quinoa Breakfast Bowls

Preparation Time: 10 minutes

- ✓ **Cooking Time: 4 minutes**
- ✓ **Servings: 4**

Ingredients:

- 1 cup quinoa, rinsed and drained
- 1 cucumber, chopped
- 1 red bell pepper, chopped
- 1/2 cup olives, pitted and sliced
- 1 tbsp. fresh basil, chopped
- 2 tbsp. fresh lemon juice
- 1 tsp lemon zest, grated
- 1 1/2 cups water
- Pepper

- Salt

Directions:

- Add quinoa, lemon zest, lemon juice, water, pepper, and salt into the instant pot and stir well.

- Seal pot with lid and cook on high for 4 minutes.

- Once done, allow to release pressure naturally for 10 minutes then release remaining using quick release. Remove lid.

- Add remaining ingredients and stir well.

- Serve immediately and enjoy it.

Nutrition:

- Calories: 199 g

- Fat: 4.6 g

- Carbohydrates: 33.6 g

- Sugar: 3 g

- Protein: 7 g

- Cholesterol: 0 mg

8. Delicious Breakfast Potato Mix

- ✓ **Preparation Time: 10 minutes**
- ✓ **Cooking Time: 15 minutes**
- ✓ **Servings: 6**

Ingredients:

- 5 potatoes, peeled and cut into wedges
- 3/4 cup mozzarella cheese, shredded
- 1 1/2 tbsp. fresh basil, chopped
- 1/2 cup sour cream
- 2 tbsp. olive oil
- 1/2 cup onion, chopped
- 1/4 cup vegetable stock
- Pepper

- Salt

Directions:

1. Add oil into the inner pot of instant pot and set the pot on sauté mode.

2. Add onion and sauté for 2-3 minutes.

3. Add potatoes, vegetable stock, pepper, and salt and stir well.

4. Seal pot with lid and cook on high for 12 minutes.

5. Once done, allow to release pressure naturally for 10 minutes then release remaining using quick release. Remove lid.

6. Add remaining ingredients and stir well.

7. Serve and enjoy.

Nutrition:

- Calories: 218 g
- Fat: 9.5 g
- Carbohydrates: 29.8 g
- Sugar: 2.5 g
- Protein: 4.7 g Cholesterol: 10 mg

9. Perfect Breakfast Oatmeal

Preparation Time: 10 minutes

- ✓ **Cooking Time: 4 minutes**
- ✓ **Servings: 4**

Ingredients:

- 1 cup steel-cut oats
- 3/4 cup unsweetened shredded coconut
- 1/4 tsp ground ginger
- 1/4 tsp ground nutmeg
- 1/2 tsp ground cinnamon
- 1/4 cup raisins
- 1 apple, chopped
- 1 1/2 cup carrots, shredded
- 1 cup unsweetened almond milk

- 3 cups of water

Directions:

1. Add all ingredients except raisins and shredded coconut into the instant pot and stir well.

2. Seal pot with lid and cook on high for 4 minutes.

3. Once done, allow to release pressure naturally. Remove lid.

4. Stir well and top with raisins and shredded coconut and serve.

Nutrition:

- Calories: 297
- Fat: 14.4 g
- Carbohydrates: 38.2 g
- Sugar: 14.9 g
- Protein: 5.2 g
- Cholesterol: 0 mg

10. Mix Berry Oatmeal

Preparation Time: 10 minutes

✓ **Cooking Time: 4 minutes**

✓ **Servings: 4**

Ingredients:

- 1 cup steel-cut oats
- 1/4 tsp ground cinnamon
- 1/2 tsp extract
- 2 tbsp. maple syrup
- 3.5 Kg fresh mixed berries
- 14.5 oz. coconut milk

Directions:

1. Spray instant pot from inside with cooking spray.

2. Add all ingredients into the inner pot of instant pot and stir well.

3. Seal pot with lid and cook on high for 4 minutes.

4. Once done, allow to release pressure naturally for 10 minutes then release remaining using quick release. Remove lid.

5. Stir well and serve.

Nutrition:

- Calories: 412
- Fat :26.3 g
- Carbohydrates: 41.3 g
- Sugar: 18.4 g
- Protein: 5.9 g
- Cholesterol: 0 mg

11. Warm Pumpkin Oats

- ✓ **Preparation Time: 10 minutes**
- ✓ **Cooking Time: 10 minutes**
- ✓ **Servings: 4**

Ingredients:

- 1 cup steel-cut oats
- 1/4 tsp ground cinnamon
- 2 1/2 tbsp. maple syrup
- 2 cups unsweetened almond milk
- 1/4 cup pumpkin puree
- 1 cup pumpkin coffee creamer
- Pinch of salt

Directions:

1. Spray instant pot from inside with cooking spray.

2. Add oats, almond milk, coffee creamer, and salt into the instant pot and stir well.

3. Seal pot with a lid and select manual, and set timer for 10 minutes.

4. Once done, allow to release pressure naturally for 10 minutes then release remaining using quick release. Remove lid.

5. Add remaining ingredients and stir well.

6. Serve and enjoy.

Nutrition:

- Calories: 139
- Fat: 3.5 g
- Carbohydrates: 26 g
- Sugar: 9.5 g
- Protein: 3.4 g
- Cholesterol: 0 mg

12. Blueberry Breakfast Oatmeal

- ✓ **Preparation Time: 10 minutes**
- ✓ **Cooking Time: 3 minutes**
- ✓ **Servings: 4**

Ingredients:

- 1 cup steel-cut oats
- 1 tbsp. maple syrup
- 3 cups of water
- 3/4 cup fresh blueberries
- Pinch of salt

Directions:

1. Spray instant pot from inside with cooking spray.
2. Add all ingredients into the inner pot of the instant pot and stir well.
3. Seal pot with lid and cook on high for 3 minutes.
4. Once done, allow to release pressure naturally. Remove lid. Stir well and serve.

Nutrition: Calories: 106 Fat: 1.4 g Carbohydrates: 21.1 g Sugar: 5.9 g Protein: 2.9 g Cholesterol: 0 mg

13. Pear Oatmeal

Preparation Time: 10 miutes

✓ **Cooking Time: 13 minutes**

✓ **Servings: 4**

Ingredients:

- 1 cup steel-cut oatmeal
- 2 cups of water
- 1/4 tsp
- 2 tbsp. maple syrup
- 1 1/4 tsp pumpkin pie spice
- 2 pears, peeled and diced
- Pinch of salt

Directions:

1. Spray instant pot from inside with cooking spray.

2. Add pears, pumpkin pie spice, and maple syrup into the instant pot and stir well and cook on sauté mode for 2 minutes.

3. Add remaining ingredients and stir well.

4. Seal pot with a lid and select manual, and set timer for 10 minutes.

5. Once done, allow to release pressure naturally for 10 minutes, then release remaining using quick release. Remove lid.

6. Stir well and serve.

Nutrition:

- Calories: 89
- Fat: 1 g
- Carbohydrates: 29.8 g
- Sugar: 16.2 g
- Protein: 1.7 g
- Cholesterol: 0 mg

The Mediterranean Diet Cookbook

Chapter 6. Lunch Recipes
14. Pumpkin Pie Parfait

- ✓ **Preparation Time: 5 minutes**
- ✓ **Cooking Time: 0 minutes**
- ✓ **Servings: 4**

Ingredients:

- 1 (15-ounce / 425-g) can pure pumpkin purée
- 4 teaspoons honey
- 1 teaspoon pumpkin pie spice
- ¼ teaspoon ground cinnamon
- 2 cups plain Greek yogurt
- 1 cup honey granola

Directions:

1. Combine the pumpkin purée, honey, pumpkin pie spice, and cinnamon in a large bowl and stir to mix well.

2. Cover the bowl with plastic wrap and chill in the refrigerator for at least 2 hours.

3. Make the parfaits: Layer each parfait glass with ¼ cup pumpkin mixture in the bottom. Top with ¼ cup of yogurt and scatter each top with ¼ cup of honey granola. Repeat the layers until the glasses are full.

4. Serve immediately.

Tip: If you want to make it a gluten-free dish, be sure to use gluten-free honey granola.

Nutrition:

- Calories: 263
- Fat: 8.9g
- Protein: 15.3g
- Carbs: 34.6g
- Fiber: 6.0g
- Sodium: 91mg

15. Mediterranean Eggs (Shakshuka)

Preparation Time: 5 minutes

Cooking Time: 20 minutes

Servings: 4

Ingredients:

- 2 tablespoons extra-virgin olive oil
- 1 cup chopped shallots
- 1 teaspoon garlic powder
- 1 cup finely diced potato
- 1 cup chopped red bell peppers
- 1 (14.5-ounce/ 411-g) can diced tomatoes, drained
- ¼ teaspoon ground cardamom
- ¼ teaspoon paprika

- ¼ teaspoon turmeric
- 4 large eggs
- ¼ cup chopped fresh cilantro

Directions:

1. Preheat the oven to 350°F (180°C).

2. Heat the olive oil in an ovenproof skillet over medium-high heat until it shimmers.

3. Add the shallots and sauté for about 3 minutes, occasionally stirring, until fragrant.

4. Fold in the garlic powder, potato, and bell peppers and stir to combine.

5. Cover and cook for 10 minutes, stirring frequently.

6. Add the tomatoes, cardamon, paprika, and turmeric and mix well.

7. When the mixture begins to bubble, remove from the heat, and crack the eggs into the skillet.

8. Transfer the skillet to the preheated oven and bake for 5 to 10 minutes, or until the egg whites are set, and the yolks are cooked to your liking.

9. Remove from the oven and garnish with the cilantro before serving.

Tip: If you prefer a spicy shakshuka, you can stir in ¼ teaspoon red pepper flakes to the tomatoes.

Nutrition:

- Calories: 223g
- Fat: 11.8g
- Protein: 9.1g
- Carbs: 19.5g
- Fiber: 3.0g
- Sodium: 277mg

16. Morning Overnight Oats with Raspberries

✓ **Preparation Time: 5 minutes**

✓ **Cooking Time: 0 minutes**

✓ **Servings: 2**

Ingredients:

- ⅔ cup unsweetened almond milk
- ¼ cup raspberries
- ⅓ cup rolled oats
- 1 teaspoon honey
- ¼ teaspoon turmeric
- ⅛ Teaspoon ground cinnamon
- Pinch ground cloves

Directions:

1. Place the almond milk, raspberries, rolled oats, honey, turmeric, cinnamon, and cloves in a mason jar. Cover and shake to combine.

2. Transfer to the refrigerator for at least 8 hours, preferably 24 hours.

3. Serve chilled.

Tip: For added crunch and flavor, you can serve it with any of your favorite toppings, such as chopped nuts, shredded coconut, or fruits.

Nutrition:

- Calories: 81 g
- Fat: 1.9g
- Protein: 2.1g
- Carbs: 13.8g
- Fiber: 3.0g
- Sodium: 97mg

17. Scramble Eggs With Tomatoes

✓ **Preparation Time: 10 minutes**

✓ **Cooking Time: 20 minutes**

✓ **Servings: 4**

Ingredients:

- 2 tablespoons extra-virgin olive oil
- ¼ cup finely minced red onion
- 1½ cups chopped fresh tomatoes
- 2 garlic cloves, minced
- ½ teaspoon dried thyme
- ½ teaspoon dried oregano
- 8 large eggs
- ½ teaspoon salt
- ¼ teaspoon freshly ground black pepper

- ¾ cup crumbled feta cheese
- ¼ cup chopped fresh mint leaves

Directions:

1. Heat the olive oil in a large skillet over medium heat.

2. Sauté the red onion and tomatoes in the hot skillet for 10 to 12 minutes, or until the tomatoes are softened.

3. Stir in the garlic, thyme, and oregano and sauté for 2 to 4 minutes, or until the garlic is fragrant.

4. Meanwhile, beat the eggs with the salt and pepper in a medium bowl until frothy.

5. Pour the beaten eggs into the skillet and reduce the heat to low—scramble for 3 to 4 minutes, stirring frequently, or until the eggs are set.

6. Remove from the heat and scatter with the feta cheese and mint. Serve warm.

Tips: For an extra dose of micronutrients, try adding sautéed kale or spinach to this tomato and egg scramble. And fresh herbs (1 to 2 teaspoons) will work just as well as dried in this dish.

Nutrition: Calories: 260 g Fat: 21.9g Protein: 10.2g Carbs: 5.8g Fiber: 1.0g Sodium: 571mg

18. Baked Eggs in Avocado

✓ **Preparation Time: 5 minutes**

✓ **Cooking Time: 10 to 15 minutes**

✓ **Servings: 2**

Ingredients:

- 1 large ripe avocado
- 2 large eggs
- Salt and freshly ground black pepper, to taste
- 4 tablespoons jarred pesto, for serving
- 2 tablespoons chopped tomato, for serving
- 2 tablespoons crumbled feta cheese, for serving (optional)

Directions:

1. Preheat the oven to 425°F (220°C).
2. Slice the avocado in half, remove the pit and scoop out a generous tablespoon of flesh from each half to create a hole big enough to fit an egg.
3. Transfer the avocado halves (cut-side up) to a baking sheet.

4. Crack 1 egg into each avocado half and sprinkle with salt and pepper.

5. Bake in the preheated oven for 10 to 15 minutes, or until the eggs are cooked to your preferred doneness.

6. Remove the avocado halves from the oven. Scatter each avocado half evenly with the jarred pesto, chopped tomato, and crumbled feta cheese (if desired). Serve immediately.

Tip: To add more flavors to this breakfast, you can serve it with your favorite toppings like fresh vegetables or a dollop of plain Greek yogurt.

Nutrition:

- Calories: 301
- Fat: 25.9g
- Protein: 8.1g
- Carbs: 9.8g
- Fiber: 5.0g
- Sodium: 435mg

19. Eggplant Parmesan

✓ **Preparation Time: 30 minutes**

✓ **Cooking Time: 1 Hour, 20 minutes**

✓ **Servings: 6**

Ingredients:

- 2 cups bread crumbs
- 1 teaspoon dried oregano
- ¼ teaspoon salt
- 1 cup skim milk
- 12 small or 6 medium eggplants, cut into ½-inch-thick slices
- 3 cups Basic Tomato Basil Sauce, or store-bought
- 4 cups diced fresh mozzarella cheese
- 1 cup freshly grated Parmesan cheese

Directions:

1. Preheat the oven to 375°F.

2. In a large bowl, stir together the bread crumbs, oregano, and salt. Pour the milk into another large bowl.

3. Dip the eggplant slices in the milk and then in the bread crumb mixture. Place the coated eggplant slices on a baking sheet.

4. Bake for 30 minutes. Remove and set aside.

5. Spread a few spoonfuls of the tomato sauce on the bottom of a 9-by-13-inch baking dish. Arrange half the eggplant over the sauce. Cover the eggplant with the mozzarella cheese. Top with the remaining eggplant. Spoon the remaining tomato sauce over the eggplant. Cover the sauce with the Parmesan cheese.

6. Bake for 40 minutes. Let rest for 10 minutes before serving.

Substitution Tip: Using gluten-free bread crumbs is an easy way to make this a gluten-free dish.

Nutrition: Calories: 490g Total Fat: 22g Saturated Fat: 13g Carbohydrates: 46g Fiber: 14g Protein: 31g Sodium: 654mg

20. Mushroom Pastilla

✓ **Preparation Time: 30 minutes**

✓ **Cooking Time: 35 minutes**

✓ **Servings: 4**

Ingredients:

- 3 large eggs
- ¼ cup olive oil
- 1 onion, chopped
- 1 pound mushrooms, chopped
- 1 teaspoon ground cinnamon, divided
- ½ teaspoon ground allspice
- ½ teaspoon ground ginger
- ½ teaspoon ground coriander
- ½ cup chopped fresh parsley

- 1 tablespoon freshly squeezed lemon juice
- ½ cup toasted slivered almonds
- Salt
- Freshly ground black pepper
- 8 sheets filo dough; follow the instructions on the package to prevent drying
- 4 tablespoons butter, melted
- 1 tablespoon powdered sugar

Directions:

1. Preheat the oven to 400°F.
2. In a small bowl, whisk the eggs and set aside.
3. In a skillet over medium heat, heat the olive oil.
4. Add the onion and sauté for 5 minutes or until softened. Add the mushrooms and cook for 5 minutes. Stir in ½ teaspoon of cinnamon, the allspice, ginger, coriander, parsley, and lemon juice.
5. Add the eggs to the skillet. Cook for about 3 minutes, stirring until the eggs are fully cooked.
6. Add the almonds. Season the mixture with salt and pepper and set aside.

7. One at a time, brush both sides of each filo sheet with melted butter and layer into an 8-inch round baking dish.

8. Spoon the mushroom filling in the center of the dough and spread it evenly. Fold the extra dough over the filling, making sure all the filling is covered. Brush the top with the remaining melted butter.

9. Bake for 15 to 20 minutes or until the filo is golden brown.

10. Dust with the powdered sugar and remaining ½ teaspoon of cinnamon. Serve hot.

Variation Tip: Add chopped apricots and raisins for sweeter flavors.

Nutrition:

- Calories: 507
- Total Fat: 38g
- Saturated Fat: 12g
- Carbohydrates: 33g
- Fiber: 5g
- Protein: 14g
- Sodium: 270mg

21. Fava Beans and Rice

- ✓ **Preparation Time: 10 minutes**
- ✓ **Cooking Time: 35 minutes**
- ✓ **Servings: 4**

Ingredients:

- ¼ cup olive oil
- 4 cups fresh fava beans, shelled
- 4½ cups water, plus more for drizzling
- 2 cups basmati rice
- ⅛ Teaspoon salt
- ⅛ Teaspoon freshly ground black pepper
- 2 tablespoons pine nuts, toasted
- ½ cup chopped fresh garlic chives or fresh onion chives

Directions:

1. In a large saucepan over medium heat, heat the olive oil.

2. Add the fava beans and drizzle them with a bit of water to avoid burning or sticking—Cook for 10 minutes.

3. Gently stir in the rice. Add the water, salt, and pepper. Increase the heat and bring the mixture to a boil. Cover the pan, reduce the heat to low, and simmer for 15 minutes.

4. Turn off the heat and let the mixture rest for 10 minutes before serving. Spoon onto a serving platter and sprinkle with the toasted pine nuts and chives.

Substitution Tip: Use lima beans if you cannot find fava beans.

Nutrition:

- Calories: 587g
- Total Fat: 17g
- Saturated Fat: 2g
- Carbohydrates: 97g
- Fiber: 2g
- Protein: 17g
- Sodium: 110mg

Chapter 8. Snacks Recipes

22. Marinated Olives

- ✓ **Preparation Time: 10 minutes Marinate Time: 3 Hours**
- ✓ **Cooking Time: 0 minutes**
- ✓ **Servings: 4**

Ingredients:

- ¼ cup olive oil
- ¼ cup red wine vinegar
- Grated zest of 1 lemon
- 1 teaspoon chopped fresh rosemary
- 2 cups jarred olives, drained

Directions:

1. In a medium bowl, whisk the olive oil, vinegar, lemon zest, and rosemary until blended.

2. Add the olives and gently stir to coat. Toss well and let marinate for at least 3 hours before serving.

3. Variation Tip: Add fresh lemon slices or a pinch of spice, like fennel seed or coriander seed.

Nutrition:

- Calories: 209g
- Total Fat: 21g
- Saturated Fat: 3g
- Carbohydrates: 7g
- Fiber: 3g
- Protein: 1g
- Sodium: 978mg

23. Pickled Turnips

- ✓ **Directions:**

- ✓ **Preparation Time: 15 minutes Pickling Time: 1 Week**

- ✓ **Cooking Time: 0 minutes**

- ✓ **Servings: 12**

Ingredients:

- 4 cups water

- ¼ cup salt

- 1 cup white distilled vinegar

- 1 small beet, peeled and quartered

- 1 garlic clove, peeled

- 2 pounds turnips, peeled, halved, and cut into ¼-inch half-moons

- In a medium bowl, whisk the water and salt until the salt dissolves. Whisk in the vinegar.

- Place the beet and garlic in a clean 2-quart glass jar with a tight-sealing lid. Layer the turnips on top.

- Pour the vinegar mixture over the turnips to cover them. Seal the lid tightly and let the jar sit at room temperature for 1 week.

Preparation Tip: Beets stain hands and clothes, so wear gloves and an apron when you peel and cut them.

Storage Tip: The pickles are ready to eat after 1 week, but they can be stored in the pantry for up to 1 month and kept refrigerated for up to 1 year.

Nutrition:

- Calories: 26g

- Total Fat: 0g

- Saturated Fat: 0g

- Carbohydrates: 6g

- Fiber: 1g

- Protein: 1g

- Sodium: 212mg

24. Braised Sweet Peppers

✓ **Preparation Time: 10 Minutes**

✓ **Cooking Time: 40 Minutes**

✓ **Servings: 4**

Ingredients:

- ¼ cup olive oil
- 1 red onion, thinly sliced
- 3 red bell peppers, seeded and cut into 1-inch strips
- 3 green bell peppers, seeded and cut into 1-inch strips
- 2 garlic cloves, chopped
- ¼ teaspoon cayenne pepper
- ⅛ Teaspoon salt

- ⅛ Teaspoon freshly ground black pepper
- ¼ cup vegetable broth
- 1 tablespoon chopped fresh thyme

Directions:

1. In a large saucepan over medium heat, heat the olive oil.
2. Add the red onion and cook for 5 minutes.
3. Add the red and green bell peppers, garlic, cayenne, salt, and black pepper.
4. Pour in the vegetable broth and bring the mixture to a boil. Cover the pan and reduce the heat to low. Cook for 35 minutes, occasionally stirring until the vegetables are soft but still firm.
5. Sprinkle the peppers with the thyme and serve.

Substitution Tip: Use 1 teaspoon dried thyme instead of fresh and add it when you add the cayenne.

Nutrition:

- Calories: 184 gTotal Fat: 15g
- Saturated Fat: 2gCarbohydrates: 15g
- Fiber: 4gProtein: 3g
- Sodium: 128mg

25. Caramelized Pearl Onions

✓ **Preparation Time: 5 minutes**

✓ **Cooking Time: 15 minutes**

✓ **Servings: 4**

Ingredients:

- ¼ cup olive oil
- 1 pound frozen pearl onions, thawed
- 3 tablespoons sugar
- ½ cup balsamic vinegar
- 1 tablespoon chopped fresh rosemary
- ⅛ Teaspoon salt
- ⅛ Teaspoon red pepper flakes

Directions:

1. In a medium sauté pan or skillet over medium heat, heat the olive oil.

2. Add the onions and cook for about 5 minutes until they begin to brown.

3. Add the sugar and cook for about 5 minutes more until the sugar is caramelized, gently stirring, so the onions do not stick to the pan.

4. Add the vinegar and rosemary. Cook for about 2 minutes, occasionally stirring, until a syrup forms.

5. Stir in the salt and red pepper flakes. Remove from the heat and let cool before serving.

Preparation Tip: Ever wonder how to judge when the oil in the pan is ready for your ingredients? Pour the oil into the pan, place a small slice of onion in the cold oil, turn on the heat, and when the onion starts to sizzle, the oil is ready for cooking!

Nutrition:

- Calories: 203g
- Total Fat: 14g
- Saturated Fat: 2g
- Carbohydrates: 18g
- Fiber: 1g
- Protein: 13g;
- Sodium: 89mg

26. Patatas Bravas

✓ **Preparation Time: 10 minutes**

✓ **Cooking Time: 20 minutes**

✓ **Servings: 4**

Ingredients:

- 2 cups olive oil, divided
- 1 tablespoon cayenne pepper, plus more as needed
- 2 tablespoons sweet paprika, plus more as needed
- 1 tablespoon all-purpose flour
- 1 cup vegetable broth
- 1/8 Teaspoon salt, plus more as needed
- 4 russet or Yukon Gold potatoes, peeled, cut into 1-inch cubes, and patted dry

Directions:

1. In a small saucepan over medium heat, heat ¼ cup of olive oil for about 2 minutes until warm. Remove from the heat and whisk in the cayenne, paprika, and flour until you have a paste.

2. Add the vegetable broth and salt. Return the saucepan to medium-low heat and cook the mixture for about 5 minutes, constantly stirring, until it thickens into a sauce. Taste and adjust the seasoning. Remove from the heat and set the sauce aside.

3. In a large skillet over medium heat, heat the remaining 1¾ cups of olive oil.

4. Gently add the potatoes and fry for about 10 minutes, occasionally stirring, until crispy and golden. Using a slotted spoon, transfer the potatoes to paper towels to drain. Transfer the potatoes to a serving platter and drizzle with the sauce.

Preparation Tip: You can also toss the potatoes in the olive oil, place them on a baking sheet, and bake in a 400°F oven for 30 minutes or until golden brown and fork-tender.

Nutrition:

- Calories: 394gTotal Fat: 27gSaturated Fat: 4g
- Carbohydrates: 38gFiber: 7gProtein: 6gSodium: 279mg

27. Filo-Wrapped Brie with Orange Marmalade

✓ **Preparation Time: 30 minutes**

✓ **Cooking Time: 30 minutes**

✓ **Servings: 12**

Ingredients:

- 4 tablespoons butter, melted
- 6 (18-by-14-inch) sheets frozen filo dough, thawed; follow the instruction on the package to prevent drying
- 1 (14-ounce) wheel Brie cheese, unwrapped, rind left on
- ½ cup orange marmalade
- Crackers, for serving

Directions:

1. Preheat the oven to 400°F.

2. Brush a baking sheet with melted butter. Place 1 sheet of filo dough on the baking sheet; brush it lightly with melted butter. Place another filo sheet on top; brush it lightly with melted butter. Repeat the same process until you finish with all 6 pieces of dough.

3. Place the cheese wheel in the center of the filo dough stack. Spoon and spread the orange marmalade over the cheese.

4. Gently fold the filo dough over the cheese and marmalade until the cheese is completely covered. Press gently to seal. Brush the filo bundle with the remaining melted butter.

5. Bake for 20 minutes or until golden brown. Let cool for 10 minutes and serve with crackers.

Substitution Tip: Use frozen puff pastry instead of filo dough.

Variation Tip: Instead of orange, use any marmalade flavor or jam for a different spin on this delicious recipe.

Nutrition:

- Calories: 205gTotal Fat: 14g
- Saturated Fat: 8g Carbohydrates: 14g
- Fiber: 0g Protein: 8g;
- Sodium: 288mg

28. Buttered Fava Beans

✓ **Preparation Time: 30 minutes**

✓ **Cooking Time: 15 minutes**

✓ **Servings: 4**

Ingredients:

- ½ cup vegetable broth
- 4 pounds fava beans, shelled
- ¼ cup fresh tarragon, divided
- 1 teaspoon chopped fresh thyme
- ¼ teaspoon freshly ground black pepper
- ⅛ Teaspoon salt
- 2 tablespoons butter
- 1 garlic clove, minced
- 2 tablespoons chopped fresh parsley

Directions:

1. In a shallow pan over medium heat, bring the vegetable broth to a boil.

2. Add the fava beans, 2 tablespoons of tarragon, the thyme, pepper, and salt. Cook for about 10 minutes until the broth is almost absorbed and the beans are tender.

3. Stir in the butter, garlic, and remaining 2 tablespoons of tarragon. Cook for 2 to 3 minutes.

4. Sprinkle with the parsley and serve hot.

Variation Tip: If you cannot find fresh fava beans, use frozen, shelled lima beans instead. Just thaw and follow the recipe as written.

Nutrition:

- Calories: 458g
- Total Fat: 9g
- Saturated Fat: 4g
- Carbohydrates: 81g
- Fiber: 0g
- Protein: 37g
- Sodium: 230mg

29. Fried Rice Balls With Tomato Sauce

- ✓ **Preparation Time: 15 minutes**
- ✓ **Cooking Time: 20 minutes**
- ✓ **Servings: Makes 8 Balls**

Ingredients:

- 1 cup bread crumbs
- 2 cups cooked risotto (see tip)
- 2 large eggs, divided
- ¼ cup freshly grated Parmesan cheese
- 8 fresh baby mozzarella balls, or 1 (4-inch) log fresh mozzarella, cut into 8 pieces
- 2 tablespoons water
- 1 cup of corn oil
- 1 cup Basic Tomato Basil Sauce, or store-bought

Directions:

1. Pour the bread crumbs into a small bowl and set aside.

2. In a medium bowl, stir together the risotto, 1 egg, and the Parmesan cheese until well.

3. Moisten your hands with a little water to prevent sticking and divide the risotto mixture into 8 pieces. Place them on a clean work surface and flatten each piece.

4. Place 1 mozzarella ball on each flattened rice disk. Close the rice around the mozzarella to form a ball. Repeat until you finish all the balls.

5. In the same medium, now-empty bowl, whisk the remaining egg and the water.

6. Dip each prepared risotto ball into the egg wash and roll it in the bread crumbs. Set aside.

7. In a large sauté pan or skillet over high heat, heat the corn oil for about 3 minutes.

8. Gently lower the risotto balls into the hot oil and fry for 5 to 8 minutes until golden brown. Stir them, as needed, to ensure the entire surface is fried. Using a slotted spoon, transfer the fried balls to paper towels to drain.

9. In a medium saucepan over medium heat, heat the tomato sauce for 5 minutes, stirring occasionally, and serve the warm sauce alongside the rice balls.

Ingredient Tip: You can prepare the Asparagus Risotto for this recipe. Follow the instructions as written, but don't add the asparagus.

Nutrition:

- Calories: 255g
- Total Fat: 15g
- Saturated Fat: 6g
- Carbohydrates: 16g
- Fiber: 2g
- Protein: 11g
- Sodium: 290mg

30. Savory Mediterranean Popcorn

✓ **Preparation Time: 5 minutes**

✓ **Cooking Time: 2 minutes**

✓ **Servings: 4 to 6**

Ingredients:

- 3 tablespoons extra-virgin olive oil
- ¼ teaspoon garlic powder
- ¼ teaspoon freshly ground black pepper
- ¼ teaspoon of sea salt
- ⅛ Teaspoon dried thyme
- ⅛ Teaspoon dried oregano
- 12 cups plain popped popcorn

Directions:

1. In a large sauté pan or skillet, heat the oil over medium heat until shimmering. Then, add the garlic powder, pepper, salt, thyme, and oregano until fragrant.

2. In a large bowl, drizzle the oil over the popcorn, toss, and serve.

Variation Tip: Make this dish fun with color by adding ⅛ teaspoon paprika to the blend for a red-tinted snack.

Nutrition:

- Calories: 183 g
- Protein: 3g
- Total Carbohydrates: 19g
- Sugars: 0g
- Fiber: 4g
- Total Fat: 12g
- Saturated Fat: 2g
- Cholesterol: 0mg
- Sodium: 146mg

31. Turkish-Spiced Nuts

✓ **Preparation Time: 10 minutes**

✓ **Cooking Time: 5 minutes**

✓ **Servings: 4 to 6**

Ingredients:

- 1 tablespoon extra-virgin olive oil
- 1 cup mixed nuts (walnuts, almonds, cashews, peanuts)
- 2 tablespoons paprika
- 1 tablespoon dried mint
- ½ tablespoon ground cinnamon
- ½ tablespoon kosher salt
- ¼ tablespoon garlic powder
- ¼ teaspoon freshly ground black pepper
- ⅛ Tablespoon ground cumin

Directions:

1. In a small to a medium saucepan, heat the oil on low heat.

2. Once the oil is warm, add the nuts, paprika, mint, cinnamon, salt, garlic powder, pepper, and cumin and stir continually until the spices are well incorporated with the nuts.

3. Preparation Tip: Blend the above spices ahead of time to cut your prep time in half.

Nutrition:

- Calories: 204

- Protein: 6g

- Total Carbohydrates: 10g

- Sugars: 2g

- Fiber: 4g

- Total Fat: 18g

- Saturated Fat: 2g

- Cholesterol: 0mg

- Sodium: 874mg

32. Lemony Orzo

✓ **Preparation Time: 5 minutes**

✓ **Cooking Time: 5 minutes**

✓ **Servings: 2 Cups**

Ingredients:

- 1 cup dry orzo
- 1 cup halved grape tomatoes
- 1 (6-ounce) bag baby spinach
- 2 tablespoons extra-virgin olive oil
- ¼ teaspoon salt
- Freshly ground black pepper
- ¾ cup crumbled feta cheese
- 1 lemon, juiced and zested

Directions:

1. Bring a medium pot of water to a boil. Stir in the orzo and cook uncovered for 8 minutes. Drain the water, then return the orzo to medium heat.

2. Add in the tomatoes and spinach and cook until the spinach is wilted. Add the oil, salt, and pepper and mix well. Top the dish with feta, lemon juice, and lemon zest, then toss one or two more times and enjoy!

3. Variation Tip: For additional fiber and protein, try whole-wheat orzo. You can even find gluten-free orzo for a gluten-free version of this dish.

Nutrition:

- Calories: 610 g
- Protein: 21g
- Total Carbohydrates: 74g
- Sugars: 6g
- Fiber: 6g
- Total Fat: 27g
- Saturated Fat: 10g
- Cholesterol: 50mg
- Sodium: 990mg

33. Puff Pastry Turnover with Roasted Vegetables

✓ **Preparation Time: 10 minutes**

✓ **Cooking Time: 35 minutes**

✓ **Servings: 4 to 6**

Ingredients:

- Nonstick cooking spray
- 1 zucchini, cut in ¼-inch-thick slices
- ½ bunch asparagus, cut into quarters
- 1 package (6-inch) whole-grain pastry discs, in the freezer section (Goya brand preferred), at room temperature
- 1 large egg, beaten

Directions:

1. Preheat the oven to 350°F.

2. Spray a baking sheet with cooking spray and arrange the zucchini and asparagus on it in a single layer. Roast for 15 to 20 minutes, until tender. Set aside to cool.

3. Allow the pastry dough to warm to room temperature. Place the discs on a floured surface.

4. Place a roasted zucchini slice on one half of each disc, then top with asparagus. Fold the empty side over the full side and pinch the turnover closed with a fork.

5. Once all discs are full and closed, brush the turnovers with the beaten egg and put them onto a baking sheet. Bake for 10 to 15 minutes, until golden brown. Let cool completely before eating.

Substitution Tip: If zucchini and asparagus aren't to your liking, try using roasted peppers and onions. You can customize these to suit anyone's palate.

Nutrition: Calories: 334g Protein: 9g Total Carbohydrates: 42g Sugars: 3g Fiber: 4g Total Fat: 15g Saturated Fat: 8g Cholesterol: 47mg Sodium: 741mg

34. Turmeric-Spiced Crunchy Chickpeas

✓ **Preparation Time: 15 minutes**

✓ **Cooking Time: 30 minutes**

✓ **Servings: 4**

Ingredients:

- 2 (15-ounce) cans organic chickpeas, drained and rinsed
- 3 tablespoons extra-virgin olive oil
- 2 teaspoons Turkish or smoked paprika
- 2 teaspoons turmeric
- ½ teaspoon dried oregano
- ½ teaspoon salt
- ¼ teaspoon ground ginger
- ⅛ Teaspoon ground white pepper (optional)

Directions:

1. Preheat the oven to 400°F. Line a baking sheet with parchment paper and set aside.

2. Completely dry the chickpeas. Lay the chickpeas out on a baking sheet, roll them around with paper towels, and allow them to air-dry. I usually let them dry for at least 2½ hours, but can also be left to dry overnight.

3. In a medium bowl, combine the olive oil, paprika, turmeric, oregano, salt, ginger, and white pepper (if using).

4. Add the dry chickpeas to the bowl and toss to combine.

5. Put the chickpeas on the prepared baking sheet and cook for 30 minutes, or until the chickpeas turn golden brown. At 15 minutes, move the chickpeas around on the baking sheet to avoid burning. Check every 10 minutes in case the chickpeas begin to crisp up before the full cooking time has elapsed.

6. Remove from the oven and set them aside to cool.

Ingredient Tip: My recipe uses canned chickpeas. A less-processed approach would be to cook beans from their dried state. You can soak 8 ounces of dried chickpeas overnight, with cold water covering the beans by 3 inches; be sure to add a tablespoon of kosher salt and, if you'd like, add some dried herbs (like oregano or bay leaf). When you're ready to cook, drain the chickpeas and simmer them in salted water for about an hour or until desired tenderness is achieved.

Nutrition:

- Calories: 308

- Protein: 11g

- Total Carbohydrates: 40g

- Sugars: <1g

- Fiber: 11g

- Total Fat: 13g

- Saturated Fat: 2g

- Cholesterol: 0mg

- Sodium: 292mg

35.   -Crispy Garlic Oven Potatoes

✓ **Preparation Time: 30 minutes**

✓ **Cooking Time: 30 minutes**

✓ **Servings: 2**

Ingredients:

- 10 ounces golden mini potatoes, halved
- 4 tablespoons extra-virgin olive oil
- 2 teaspoons dried, minced garlic
- 1 teaspoon onion salt
- ½ teaspoon paprika
- ¼ teaspoon freshly ground black pepper
- ¼ teaspoon red pepper flakes
- ¼ teaspoon dried dill

Directions:

1. Preheat the oven to 400°F.

2. Soak the potatoes and put in a bowl of ice water for 30 minutes. Change the water if you return, and the water is milky.

3. Rinse and dry the potatoes, then put them on a baking sheet.

4. Drizzle the potatoes with oil and sprinkle with the garlic, onion salt, paprika, pepper, red pepper flakes, and dill. Using tongs or your hands, toss well to coat.

5. Lower the heat to 375°F, add potatoes to the oven, and bake for 20 minutes.

6. At 20 minutes, check and flip potatoes. Bake for another 10 minutes, or until the potatoes are fork-tender.

Substitution Tip: Swap sweet potatoes for the golden mini potatoes for a sweeter twist on this savory dish.

Nutrition: Calories: 344g Protein: 3gTotal Carbohydrates: 24g Sugars: 1g Fiber: 4g Total Fat: 28g Saturated Fat: 4g Cholesterol: 0mg Sodium: 723mg

Chapter 10. Dinner Recipes

36. Naked Lasagna

- ✓ **Preparation Time: 15 minutes**
- ✓ **Cooking Time: 10 minutes**
- ✓ **Servings: 4**

Ingredients:

- 8 oz. whole-wheat rotini
- 3 sliced garlic cloves
- 8 c. baby spinach
- 8 oz. sliced white mushrooms
- 1 chopped onion
- 14 oz. diced tomatoes

- ¾ c. ricotta cheese
- ½ tsp. crushed red pepper
- ½ tsp. Salt
- ¼ tsp. Pepper

Directions:

1. Place water in a large pot and boil, and add in the pasta. You will want to cook for 8 to 10 minutes or until the pasta is tender.

2. In a large skillet, place your onions and garlic over medium heat and cook until they begin to brown. This should take around 3 minutes.

3. Once the time has passed, add in the mushrooms and the salt and pepper and stir for 4 to 6 minutes.

4. When this is done, add in the spinach, tomatoes, and crushed red pepper. Increase your heat to medium-high and cook for about 4 minutes.

5. Last, you will want to add the sauce with the pasta and add the ricotta cheese for a final touch.

Nutrition:

- Calories: 370g Protein: 18g Carbs: 47g Fat: 13g

37. Gnocchi, Tomatoes, and Pancetta

✓ **Preparation Time: 10 minutes**

✓ **Cooking Time: 7 minutes**

✓ **Servings: 4**

Ingredients:

- 1 lb. gnocchi
- 4 oz. watercress
- 2 oz. pancetta
- 2 chopped tomatoes
- 3 minced garlic cloves
- 2 tsp. Red-wine vinegar
- ¼ tsp. Crushed red pepper
- ½ tsp. Sugar

- ¼ tsp. salt
- 1/3 c. grated Parmesan cheese

Directions:

1. Place water in a large pot and bring to a boil.

2. You will want to cook the pancetta for about 5 minutes in a large skillet over medium heat.

3. Once it has changed color, add in the garlic and cook the mixture for another 30 seconds.

4. When the garlic is simmering, add the crushed red pepper, sugar, and tomatoes for 5 minutes.

5. Last, stir in the vinegar and salt and then remove the mixture from the heat.

6. In the boiling pot of water, place the gnocchi and cook for 3 to 5 minutes or until it is floating.

7. Drain the gnocchi over the watercress and then add the gnocchi to the sauce in the pan. Be sure to toss it well to make sure all of the ingredients are combined. Last, dish the meal into separate plates and decorate with Parmesan cheese if desired.

Nutrition: Calories: 377g Protein: 14g Carbs: 64g Fat: 7g

38. Penne and Chicken

✓ **Preparation Time: 15 minutes**

✓ **Cooking Time: 10 minutes**

✓ **Servings: 4**

Ingredients:

- 16 oz. penne noodles
- 1 ½ tbsps. Butter
- ½ c. red onion, chopped
- 2 minced garlic cloves
- 1 lb. boneless and skinless chicken breast.
- 14 oz. chopped artichoke hearts, drained
- 1 chopped tomato
- ½ c. feta cheese, crumbled

- 3 tbsps. Chopped parsley
- 2 tbsps. Lemon juice
- 1 tsp. dried oregano
- Salt
- Pepper

Directions:

1. Place salted water in a pot and allow it to boil.
2. Add penne. Cook pasta until firm and then drain.
3. Meanwhile, warm butter in a skillet.
4. Add garlic and onion. Allow 2 minutes to cook.
5. Add in chicken and cook for 6 minutes, stirring occasionally. Once cooked, set oven to medium-low.
6. Using a skillet, add chopped artichoke hearts, parsley, dried oregano, tomato, feta cheese, lemon juice, and drained penne pasta—Cook for approximately 3 minutes.
7. Season with salt and pepper. Serve warm.

Nutrition: Calories: 330g Protein: 20g Carbs: 52g Fat: 4.5g

39. Spinach and Feta Pita Bake

✓ **Preparation Time: 15 minutes**

✓ **Cooking Time: 10-12 minutes**

✓ **Servings: 6**

Ingredients:

- 6 oz. tomato pesto
- 6 whole-wheat pita bread
- 2 chopped tomatoes
- 1 bunch chopped spinach
- 4 sliced mushrooms
- ½ c. crumbled feta cheese
- 2 tbsps. Grated Parmesan cheese
- 3 tbsps. Olive oil

Directions:

1. Set oven to 350 º F

2. Spread tomato pesto onto one side of each pita bread and place them pesto-side up on a baking sheet.

3. Top pitas with spinach, tomatoes, mushrooms, feta cheese, and Parmesan cheese.

4. Sprinkle with olive oil, and add pepper for seasoning.

5. Bake in preheated oven for 10-12 minutes or until pitas are crisp. Cut into quarters and serve.

Nutrition:

- Fat: 11g
- Carbs: 41g
- Protein: 17g
- Calories 350g

40. Mediterranean Flounder

✓ **Preparation Time: 15 minutes**

✓ **Cooking Time: 15 minutes**

✓ **Servings: 4**

Ingredients:

- 5 plum tomatoes
- 2 tbsps. Olive oil
- ½ chopped Spanish onion
- 2 chopped garlic cloves
- 1 tsp. Italian seasoning
- 24 Kalamata olives
- ¼ c. white wine
- ¼ c. capers
- 1 tsp. fresh lemon juice

- 6 leaves of basil
- 3 tbsps. Grated Parmesan cheese
- 1 lb. flounder fillets
- 6 leaves basil

Directions:

1. Set oven to 425 °F

2. Then bring a saucepan of water to a boil. Add tomatoes and immediately remove, place in a medium bowl of ice water, then drain. Remove and discard skins from tomatoes. Chop, and then set aside.

3. In a skillet, warm olive oil. Add onion and cook until tender. Stir in tomatoes, garlic, and Italian seasoning. Cook until tomatoes are soft, 5-7 minutes.

4. Then mix in wine, capers, olives, ½ of the basil, and lemon juice. Reduce heat and stir in Parmesan cheese. Cook for approximately 15 mins until the mixture is reduced to a thick sauce.ine a shallow baking dish with your flounder filets. Pour your sauce over the fillets and top with the rest of the basil.Bake for about 12 minutes or until the fish is easily flaked with a fork.

Nutrition: Calories: 282g Protein: 24g Carbs: 8.1g Fat: 15.4g

41. Greek Olive and Feta Cheese Pasta

- ✓ **Preparation Time: 90 minutes**
- ✓ **Cooking Time: 15 minutes**
- ✓ **Servings: 4**

Ingredients:

- 2 cloves of finely minced fresh garlic
- 2 large tomatoes, seeded and diced
- 3 oz. feta cheese, crumbled
- ½ diced red bell pepper
- 10 small-sized Greek olives, coarsely chopped and pitted
- ½ diced yellow bell pepper
- ¼ cup basil leaves, coarsely chopped
- 1 Tbsp. Olive oil

- ¼ tsp hot pepper, finely chopped
- 4 ½ oz. of ziti pasta

Directions:

1. Cook pasta to a desirable point, drain it, sprinkle with olive oil, and set aside.

2. In a large bowl, mix olives, feta cheese, basil, garlic, and hot pepper. Leave for 30 minutes.

3. To the same bowl, add the cooked pasta, the bell peppers, and toss. Refrigerate for up to an hour. Toss again, then serve chilled.

Nutrition:

- Calories: **235 kcal**
- Carbs: **27g**
- Fat: **10g**
- Protein: 7g.

42. Tomatoes Stuffed With Goat Cheese

✓ **Preparation Time: 15 minutes**

✓ **Cooking Time: 0 minutes**

✓ **Servings: 2**

Ingredients:

- 1 tsp. Extra Virgin Olive oil
- Parsley, freshly chopped
- 3 oz. feta cheese
- 7 Arugula leaves
- Salt, to taste
- Freshly grounded pepper, to taste
- ¼ tsp balsamic vinegar
- 1 red onion, thinly sliced

- 2 medium-sized ripe tomatoes

Directions:

1. Put 3-4 arugula leaves at the center of the two salad plates.

2. Slice ¼ inches off the top of each tomato. Core ½ inch off the center of each tomato.

3. Fill the space in the tomatoes with feta cheese, salt, and pepper to the desired taste.

4. Drizzle each tomato with olive oil and balsamic vinegar

5. Garnish the top with slices of red onion and parsley. It is done.

Nutrition:

- Calories: 142 kcal
- Carbs: 7g
- Fat: 13g
- Protein: 7g

43. Cucumber Yogurt Salad

- ✓ **Preparation Time: 10 minutes**
- ✓ **Cooking Time: 0 minutes**
- ✓ **Servings: 4**

Ingredients:

- 2 peeled and diced English cucumbers
- 1 ½ Tbsps. fresh garlic, crushed
- Pinch of Salt
- 2 tsp. dried mint
- 1/8 Tbsp. fresh dill, already minced
- 1 quart low-fat yogurt, plain

Directions:

1. In a small bowl, mix the dill, garlic, and salt.

2. Pour the yogurt in and mix well.

3. Add cucumber, mint and stir well

4. Put inside the refrigerator to chill, then serve.

Nutrition:

- Calories: 167 kcal
- Carbs: 21g
- Fat: 4g
- Protein: 13g.

44. Savory Greek White Fava Bean Salad

✓ **Preparation Time: 24 hours**

✓ **Cooking Time: 60 minutes**

✓ **Servings: 4**

Ingredients:

- 3 Tbsp. olive-oil
- 1 onion, small and finely chopped
- Salt
- 4 ½ Tbsp. red wine vinegar
- 2-3 sage leaves, fresh
- 3 Tbsp. lemon juice, freshly squeezed
- Freshly grounded pepper
- 1 celery stalk, fresh and chopped
- 1 ¼ cup dried fava beans, white

- ½ Tbsp. of oregano, dried

- 2 cloves of finely minced garlic.

Directions:

1. Beans should be soaked in a lot of water overnight

2. The next morning drain the beans and make sure to rinse it with fresh water.

3. Put drained beans into another pot of freshwater, add sage, cover the pot, and allow it to cook for about 45 minutes.

4. Add salt.

5. Cook for another 15 minutes to allow beans to become soft.

6. Drain the beans, then add lemon juice, olive oil, onion, garlic, oregano, celery, and vinegar. Add pepper to desired taste.

7. Refrigerate for an hour before serving.

Nutrition:

- Calories: 253 kcal

- Carbs: 28g

- Fat: 11g Protein: 12g

45. Tangy Orange Roasted Asparagus Salad

- ✓ **Preparation Time: 24 hours**
- ✓ **Cooking Time: 60 minutes**
- ✓ **Servings: 4**

Ingredients:

- 2 cloves of minced garlic
- 1 tsp. of basil leaf
- Salt
- 6 cups of romaine lettuce
- 1 pound of fresh asparagus
- Romano cheese preferably grated
- 4 tsp of orange juice
- 1 Tbsp. of lime juice

- 4 tsp of olive oil
- Ground pepper
- 3 tsp. of toasted pine nuts

Directions:

1. Mix asparagus and 2 tsp of olive oil, salt to desired taste

2. Put already mixed asparagus in the oven, roast for 10 minutes until it is tender crispy.

3. In another bowl, mix garlic, orange juice, 2 tsp of olive oil, lime juice, and include salt and pepper to desired taste.

4. When it ready, add lettuce to the salad, put asparagus on top of it, and add pine nuts with basil. Add Romano cheese if desired.

Nutrition:

- Calories: 253 kcal
- Carbs: 28g
- Fat: 11g
- Protein: 12g

46. Mediterranean Mixed Greens

✓ **Preparation Time: 5 minutes**

✓ **Cooking Time: 0 minutes**

✓ **Servings: 5**

Ingredients:

- ¼ cup of chopped walnuts
- Ground pepper, to taste
- 6 cups mixed greens
- ¼ cup of dried cranberries
- 1 red onion
- 20 cherry tomatoes

Directions:

1. In a big bowl, mix the onion, walnuts, tomatoes, cranberries, and green

2. Stir thoroughly. Serve

Nutrition:

- Calories: 140 kcal

- Carbs: 6g Fat: 13g

- Protein: 2.5g

47. Creamy Paninis

- ✓ **Preparation Time: 10 minutes**
- ✓ **Cooking Time: 5 minutes**
- ✓ **Servings: 4**

Ingredients:

- 1 zucchini mostly thinly sliced
- ½ cup of mayonnaise with olive oil
- 2 Tbsps. of black olives
- ¼ cup of basil leaves
- 7 oz. of roasted red pepper
- 8 slices of wheat bread
- 4 slices bacon
- 4 slices of provolone cheese

Directions:

1. Inside a bowl, mix the mayonnaise, basil, and olives. Spread the mayonnaise mixture on the bread and place 4 slices of provolone and bacon, 1 slice of zucchini and sprinkle the pepper all over. Place another piece of bread on top of it and put mayonnaise on it.

2. Butter the non-stick pan, then place the bread in and cook for about 4 minutes before you flip it to the other side.

3. Keep on heat until the sandwich is brown and the cheese is already melted.

4. Serve.

Nutrition:

- Calories: 553g
- Total Fat: 38.7g
- Cholesterol: 50mg
- Carbs: 28.1g
- Fiber: 4.8g
- Sugars: 6g
- Protein: 22.3g

Chapter 13. Drinks Recipes

48. Turkish Coffee Almond Frappé

- ✓ **Preparation Time: 10 minutes**
- ✓ **Cooking Time: 0 minutes**
- ✓ **Servings: 2**

Ingredients:

- 2½ cups cold Almond Milk (here)
- ¼ cup pure maple syrup or 4 pitted dates
- 1 tablespoon ground Turkish coffee or 2 teaspoons instant espresso powder
- Ice (optional)

Directions:

1. Combine the almond milk, maple syrup or dates, coffee, and ice (if using) in a blender. Blend until smooth.
2. Pour into two glasses and serve immediately.

Tip: You can customize this drink however you'd like by adding, cinnamon, or whole unsalted almonds, or even unsalted almond butter.

Nutrition:

- Calories: 153g
- Protein: 1g
- Total Carbohydrates: 29g
- Fiber: 1g
- Total Fat: 5g
- Saturated Fat: 0g
- Cholesterol: 0mg
- Sodium: 209mg

49. Moroccan Mint Tea

✓ **Preparation Time: 15 minutes**

✓ **Cooking Time:**

✓ **Servings: 4**

Ingredients:

- 1 tablespoon green tea leaves
- ¼ cup sugar
- 4 cups boiling water
- 1 bunch fresh mint, washed

Directions:

1. Place the tea leaves and sugar in a teapot. Add boiling water.

2. Add the mint, press it down into the water with a spoon, and let steep at least 5 minutes.

3. Pour the tea through a strainer to serve.

Tip: Make a batch, strain it into a quart jar, and chill overnight to make iced Moroccan mint tea. Serve in tall glasses garnished with fresh mint sprigs.

Nutrition:

- Calories: 48g
- Protein: 0g
- Total Carbohydrates: 13g
- Fiber: 0g
- Total Fat: 0g
- Saturated Fat: 0g
- Cholesterol: 0mg
- Sodium: 1mg

50. Chamomile Lemon Honey Iced Tea

✓ **Preparation Time: 10 minutes**

✓ **Cooking Time: 0 minutes**

✓ **Servings: 4**

Ingredients:

- 4 bags high-quality chamomile tea
- ¼ cup lemon juice
- ¼ cup honey
- 4 cups boiling water
- 4 strips lemon peel
- Ice cubes

Directions:

1. Place the chamomile, lemon, and honey in a teapot. Pour boiling water over them, and let steep for at least 5 minutes.

2. Remove the tea bags and pour the tea into a heat-tempered jar or pitcher. Chill until cold.

3. When you're ready to serve, twist strips of lemon peel to release the oils and place one strip in each serving glass. Add ice and the iced tea.

Tip: Orange juice and peel can be used instead of the lemon juice and peel for a sweeter drink. Replace the honey with pure maple syrup for a vegan drink.

Nutrition:

- Calories: 68g
- Protein: 0g,
- Total Carbohydrates: 18g,
- Fiber: 0g,
- Total Fat: 0g,
- Saturated Fat: 0g,
- Cholesterol: 0mg,
- Sodium: 4mg

51. Pomegranate Berry Sangria

- ✓ **Preparation Time: 10 minutes**
- ✓ **Cooking Time: 0 minutes**
- ✓ **Servings: 4**

Ingredients:

- 4 cups pomegranate juice
- 1 cup red wine
- ⅓ Cup honey
- ¼ cup lemon juice
- 1 cup mixed berries
- 4 strips orange peel

Directions:

1. Place the pomegranate juice, red wine, honey, lemon juice, and berries in a large serving pitcher.

2. Stir to dissolve the honey and slightly mash the berries. Chill.

3. When you're ready to serve, twist the orange peel to release the oils and place a strip of peel in each glass. Pour in the sangria and serve.

Tip: I like to serve this over ice. I also like to add a cinnamon stick to the pitcher as it chills, but I remove it to serve, since the cinnamon flavor can become too strong. To make it vegan, use sugar instead of honey.

Nutrition:

- Calories: 299 g
- Protein: 1g,
- Total Carbohydrates: 65g,
- Fiber: 1g,
- Total Fat: 0g,
- Saturated Fat: 0g,
- Cholesterol: 0mg,
- Sodium: 17mg

52. Raspberry Fizz Cocktail

✓ **Preparation Time: 10 minutes**

✓ **Cooking Time: 0 minutes**

✓ **Servings: 4**

Ingredients:

- 1 pint raspberries
- 2 tablespoons reduced-sugar raspberry jam
- 1 tablespoon lemon juice
- 2 teaspoons chopped fresh mint
- 1 bottle Prosecco, chilled

Directions:

1. Reserve 8 to 12 nice berries to float in wine glasses.

2. Place the remaining berries, raspberry jam, and lemon juice in a small bowl.

3. Using the back of a spoon or a pestle, mash the berries to release their juices and macerate them.

4. Place around 2 tablespoons of the mashed berries in each glass.

5. Add a pinch of chopped mint to each glass.

6. Gradually add the Prosecco, pouring slowly, so it doesn't overflow.

7. Stir once and serve.

Tip: You can crush the berries hours ahead or store the macerated berries in an ice cube tray in the freezer and use them frozen in this cocktail. If you can't find Prosecco in your area, any champagne or sparkling wine will work.

Nutrition:

- Calories: 204g Protein: 1g Total Carbohydrates: 18g
- Fiber: 5g Total Fat: 1g Saturated Fat: 0g
- Cholesterol: 0mg
- Sodium: 2mg

53. Chocolate Banana Smoothie

- ✓ **Preparation Time: 5 minutes**
- ✓ **Cooking Time: 0 minutes**
- ✓ **Servings:2**

Ingredients:

- 2 bananas, peeled
- 1 cup unsweetened almond milk, or skim milk
- 1 cup crushed ice
- 3 tablespoons unsweetened cocoa powder
- 3 tablespoons honey

Directions:

1. In a blender, combine the bananas, almond milk, ice, cocoa powder, and honey. Blend until smooth.

Nutrition:

- Calories: 219g
- Protein: 2g
- Total Carbohydrates: 57g
- Sugars: 40g
- Fiber: 6g
- Total Fat: 2g
- Saturated Fat: <1g
- Cholesterol: 0mg
- Sodium: 4mg

54. Fruit Smoothie

✓ **Preparation Time: 5 minutes**

✓ **Cooking Time: 0 minutes Servings:2**

Ingredients:

- 2 cups blueberries (or any fresh or frozen fruit, cut into pieces if the fruit is large)
- 2 cups unsweetened almond milk
- 1 cup crushed ice
- ½ teaspoon ground ginger (or other dried ground spice such as turmeric, cinnamon, or nutmeg)

Directions:

1. In a blender, combine the blueberries, almond milk, ice, and ginger. Blend until smooth.

Nutrition: Calories: 125g Protein: 2g Total Carbohydrates: 23g Sugars: 14g Fiber: 5g Total Fat: 4g Fat: <1g Cholesterol: 0mg Sodium: 181mg

55. Mango-Pear Smoothie

- ✓ **Preparation Time: 10 minutes**
- ✓ **Cooking Time: 0 minutes**
- ✓ **Servings: 1**

Ingredients:

- 1 ripe pear, cored and chopped
- ½ mango, peeled, pitted, and chopped
- 1 cup chopped kale
- ½ cup plain Greek yogurt
- 2 ice cubes

Directions:

1. In a blender, purée the pear, mango, kale, and yogurt.

2. Add the ice and blend until thick and smooth. Pour the smoothie into a glass and serve cold.

Nutrition:

- Calories: 293g
- Total Fat: 8g
- Saturated Fat: 5g
- Carbohydrates: 53g
- Fiber: 7g
- Protein: 8g

56. Strawberry-Rhubarb Smoothie

✓ **Preparation Time: 5 minutes**

✓ **Cooking Time: 3 minutes**

✓ **Servings: 1**

Ingredients:

- 1 rhubarb stalk, chopped
- 1 cup sliced fresh strawberries
- ½ cup plain Greek yogurt
- 2 tablespoons honey
- Pinch ground cinnamon
- 3 ice cubes

Directions:

1. Place a small saucepan filled with water over high heat and bring to a boil. Add the rhubarb and boil for 3 minutes. Drain and transfer the rhubarb to a blender.

2. Add the strawberries, yogurt, honey, and cinnamon and pulse the mixture until it is smooth.

3. Add the ice and blend until thick, with no ice lumps remaining. Pour the smoothie into a glass and enjoy cold.

Nutrition:

- Calories: 295 g
- Total Fat: 8g
- Saturated Fat: 5g
- Carbohydrates: 56g;
- Fiber: 4g
- Protein: 6g

57. Chia-Pomegranate Smoothie

- **Preparation Time: 5 minutes**
- **Difficulty Level: 2/5**
- **Cooking Time: 0 minutes**
- **Servings: 2**

Ingredients:

- 1 cup pure pomegranate juice (no sugar added)
- 1 cup frozen berries
- 1 cup coarsely chopped kale
- 2 tablespoons chia seeds
- 3 Medjool dates, pitted and coarsely chopped
- Pinch ground cinnamon

Directions:

1. In a blender, combine the pomegranate juice, berries, kale, chia seeds, dates, and cinnamon and pulse until smooth. Pour into glasses and serve.

Nutrition:

- Calories: 275g
- Total fat: 5g
- Saturated fat: 1g
- Carbohydrates: 59g
- Sugar: 10g
- Fiber: 42g
- Protein: 5g

58. Sweet Kale Smoothie

✓ **Preparation Time: 10 minutes**

✓ **Cooking Time: 15 minutes**

✓ **Servings: 2**

Ingredients:

- 1 cup low-fat plain Greek yogurt
- ½ cup apple juice
- 1 apple, cored and quartered
- 4 Medjool dates
- 3 cups packed coarsely chopped kale
- Juice of ½ lemon
- 4 ice cubes

Directions:

1. In a blender, combine the yogurt, apple juice, apple, and dates and pulse until smooth.

2. Add the kale and lemon juice and pulse until blended. Add the ice cubes and blend until smooth and thick. Pour into glasses and serve.

Nutrition:

- Calories: 355
- Total fat: 2g
- Saturated fat: 1g
- Carbohydrates: 77g
- Sugar: 58g
- Fiber: 8g
- Protein: 11g

59. Avocado-Blueberry Smoothie

✓ **Preparation Time: 5 minutes**

✓ **Cooking Time: 0 minutes**

✓ **Servings: 2**

Ingredients:

- ½ cup unsweetened almond milk
- ½ cup low-fat plain Greek yogurt
- 1 ripe avocado, peeled, pitted, and coarsely chopped
- 1 cup blueberries
- ¼ cup gluten-free rolled oats
- ½ teaspoon extract
- 4 ice cubes

Directions:

1. In a blender, combine the almond milk, yogurt, avocado, blueberries, oats, and and pulse until well blended.

2. Add the ice cubes and blend until thick and smooth. Serve.

Nutrition:

- Calories: 273g
- Total fat: 15g
- Saturated fat: 2g
- Carbohydrates: 28g
- Sugar: 10g
- Fiber: 9g
- Protein: 10g

Conclusion

The Mediterranean diet is not about following a specific set of restrictions and rules to achieve your desired results. This alone makes it easier to follow than many diet plans because it is not a diet plan but more of a way of life. The main idea behind the Mediterranean diet is to eat real food in reasonable quantities. And because it emphasizes the consumption of foods that are good for you, it is reasonable that the Mediterranean diet has many health benefits.

Following the Mediterranean diet might lower your risk of developing heart disease. Right now, heart disease is responsible for killing one out of every four Americans every year. You are more likely to die from some form of heart disease than you are to die from any other illness or accident. Some forms of heart disease are unavoidable, like congenital diseases that people are born with. But most forms of heart diseases are directly caused by or made worse by a sedentary lifestyle and poor dietary habits.

Many heart-related illnesses are caused by high blood pressure. Your blood pressure consists of two numbers: the systolic number and the diastolic number; the systolic number is the one on top. The diastolic number shows how much pressure your blood is putting on the arteries' walls in your body when your heart is at rest in between its beats. The systolic number measures the amount of pressure the blood is putting on the arteries' walls when your heart is beating. Once your systolic number is over one hundred thirty and your diastolic number is over eighty, you are considered to have problems with your blood pressure.

When the flow of blood to and from your heart is blocked, for whatever reason, then you can suffer from a heart attack. A heart attack will happen when there is a blockage in one of the coronary arteries that bring the blood back to your heart when it is full of oxygen. If the blockage can continue for very long, then the heart muscles will begin to die. A stroke is much the same thing as a heart attack, except that it happens in the arteries that lead to the brain. Like the muscles of the heart, the brain muscles can quickly die if they are deprived of oxygen for too long. And just like a heart attack, the likelihood of suffering a stroke is increased with obesity.

Diabetes can occur congenitally, such as Type One Diabetes, or a product of poor lifestyle and obesity, such as Type Two Diabetes. The second form of diabetes, which is often referred to as sugar diabetes, relates more to how your body handles sugar and not how much sugar you eat. When you eat or drink, you are consuming sugar in some form and level. Some foods naturally contain more sugar than other foods. Fruit contains fructose, which is a natural sugar but still a type of sugar. When you consume something, your brain sends a message to your pancreas to create the hormone insulin to help break down the molecules from the food and help your body use them as energy. When your body has broken down the food, it has converted them to small molecules. The insulin will then travel through the body with the food to help it get into the cells where it is needed.

When you continuously overeat or eat many processed and refined foods, the body will make more insulin to help the foods get into the cells for use as energy. The problem comes when this becomes a repeated cycle, where the pancreas needs to keep making more and more of the insulin. Over time, the cells in your body will become resistant to insulin when they are full and have no room for more molecules of energy. When that happens, the molecules will be stored as fat in various places in the body.

The risk of developing certain cancers, like pancreatic, kidney, esophageal, uterine, breast, and colorectal, increases with obesity. This is believed to be the work of visceral fat surrounding the body's major organs and affect certain necessary processes in the body. The cells of visceral fat are quite large, and there are many of them in an obese person's body. One thing that visceral fat does is prevent oxygen-rich blood from getting to the organs in the amounts needed to sustain life. This environment that is low in oxygen causes a rise in inflammation. Some inflammation is good for the body. If you have a small scrape or a cut, then the body will send white blood cells to the area to kill any bacteria in the wound. This rush of white blood cells will cause inflammation to the area, a small swelling that will go away when the infection risk is gone, and the white blood cells are no longer needed.